Theological Building Blocks
for Biblical Counseling

Dr. Nicolas Ellen

Theological Building Blocks for Biblical Counseling

Copyright © 2011 by Dr. Nicolas Ellen

All rights reserved in all countries. No part of this material may be reproduced, stored in a retrieval system, or transmitted in any form or by any means electronic, mechanical, photocopying, recording, or otherwise without prior written permission of the author, publisher and/or copyright owners, except as provided by USA copyright law.

Readers may order copies by visiting www.mycounselingcorner.com.

Published and Printed By Expository Counseling Center
Houston, Texas

Unless otherwise noted, scripture references are taken from the New American Standard Bible. © The Lockman Foundation, 1960, 1962, 1963, 1968, 1971, 1972, 1973, 1975, 1977.

Publisher's Cataloging in Publication

Ellen, Nicolas: *Theological Building Blocks for Biblical Counseling*
1. Counseling 2. Christian Counseling 3. Christianity 4. Discipleship

ISBN: 978-0-9779695-5-5

Theological Building Blocks for Biblical Counseling

Section 1	What Makes Biblical Counseling Biblical?	5
Section 2	The Theological Foundations for Biblical Counseling	12
Section 3	The Doctrine of God and Biblical Counseling	18
Section 4	The Doctrine of Christ/ Holy Spirit and Biblical Counseling	32
Section 5	The Doctrine of Truth/ Scriptures and Biblical Counseling	38
Section 6	The Doctrine of Man /Sin and Biblical Counseling	41
Section 7	The Doctrine of The Gospel/Salvation and Biblical Counseling	45
Section 8	The Doctrine of Mortification / Sanctification and Biblical Counseling	52
Section 9	The Essence of Spiritual Development /Maturity and Biblical Counseling	57
Section 10	The Doctrine of Spiritual Warfare/Sanctification Process and Biblical Counseling	66
Section 11	The Point of Choice/The Purpose of Life and Biblical Counseling	70
Section 12	Physical Illness/Christians on Psychotropic Drugs and Biblical Counseling	86
Section 13	The Need of Relationships and Biblical Counseling	93
Section 14	Understanding the Church and Biblical Counseling	101

Section One
What Makes Biblical Counseling Biblical?

Key Point: Biblical counseling can be defined as using the Word of God (the Bible) within the context it was written to provide solutions and the application of those solutions to non organic, immaterial, spiritual, and what the world calls "psychological" or "mental disorder" problems. The Word of God is used in a precise and efficient manner to address these matters, and is used anticipating the salvation of sinners and the sanctification of Saints as a result. Biblical counseling can also be defined as using the Word of God to give comprehensive answers to non-physical problems on a small group level or on a one on one interpersonal level. In essence biblical counseling is applied biblical systematic theology. It is the practical ministry that comes out of knowing and understanding the Bible and the theology of the Bible. Biblical Counseling is the practical, comprehensive ministry of soul care that comes out of knowing, understanding, and applying biblical systematic theology to life issues. Your view of counseling will be determined by your worldview. The more biblical your worldview, the more biblical your counseling. The less biblical your worldview, the less biblical your counseling will be. Your worldview is determined by those whom you have allowed to teach you. The Bible says, "No student is above his teacher but when fully trained will be like his teacher" (Luke 6:40). You must determine if your view of counseling has been shaped by teaching that is driven by Satan or teaching that is driven by the Son of God! In other words, you must evaluate your model of counseling to determine if it is biblical or unbiblical.

Eight key questions we can use to evaluate a Model of Counseling to determine if it is biblical or unbiblical

1. What are the philosophical assumptions about life and God that undergird this model of counseling (Humanism, Naturalism, Theism, etc.)?

2. What is the belief about the nature of man (model of personality) in this model of counseling?

3. What is the belief about what is wrong with mankind (model of abnormality) in this model of counseling?

4. What is the belief about what makes a healthy / whole human being (model of health) in this model of counseling?

5. What is the method (model of counseling) of leading a person to their view of a healthy / whole human being in this model of counseling?

6. What are the tangible measures (demonstrated effectiveness) to determine success in achieving their goal of a healthy / whole human being?

7. Where does this model contradict, compete with, or complement what the Bible says about life, God, the nature or man, or a healthy whole human being?

8. Where does this model contradict, compete with, or complement what the Bible says in its methodology and view of success?

Three Major Schools of Thoughts in Counseling

Psychological Counseling—combines human observations with human wisdom to construct a system of counsel to help man deal with his problems and issues of life. This type of counseling is generally practiced by non-believers and Christians who accept psychological theories as an avenue to help people.

Integration Counseling—combines human observation, human wisdom, and the Bible to construct a system of counsel to help man deal with his problems and issues of life. This is sometimes called "Christian Counseling." This type of counseling is generally practiced by Christians who believe that Bible should be supplemented with psychological theories in order to help people.

Biblical Counseling—takes the Bible to construct a system of counsel to help man deal with his non-physical or immaterial problems of life. This type of counseling is generally practiced by Christians who believe that the Bible has all we need to provide solutions to man's non-physical, or immaterial problems as well as what the world calls "psychological" problems. They also believe that the Bible can help man function as God intended in life.

1. Biblical counseling focuses on helping people deal with the heart issues that drive the behavioral issues as explained by God in His Word (James 3:13-4:10, Luke 6:43-45, Matthew 6:19-21, Ezekiel 14:1-11).

2. Biblical counseling focuses on helping people turn from sin in their thoughts, words, actions, and relationships as prescribed by God in His Word (Colossians 3:5-9, Ephesians 4:17-22, 1John 1:9, Proverbs 28:13-14).

3. Biblical counseling focuses on helping people walk in Christ's Righteousness in their thoughts, words, actions, and relationships as prescribed by God in His Word (Galatians 5:16-25, Ephesians 4:23-32, Colossians 3:10-25, Romans 12:1-3).

4. Biblical counseling facilitates the process of one becoming like Christ in all aspects of life (Ephesians 4:11-16, Colossians 1:28-29).

5. Biblical Counseling leads a person into truth that comes from God and not human observations and theories that are an antithesis to Scripture (Matthew 28:18-20, 1Timothy 6:3-6, 2Peter 1:16-21).

6. Biblical Counseling leads unbelievers to Christ as it shares with unbelievers their ultimate problem (sin) and their true need salvation (2Corinthians 5:15-21).

7. Biblical Counseling helps individuals in the Body of Christ grow spiritually as it focuses on their real problem—sin—and their solution—Putting off sin and Putting on Righteousness (Ephesians 4:17-32, 2Peter 1:1-10).

8. Biblical Counseling provides the community with God's Solutions to life's immaterial, non-physical, or what world calls "psychological" problems (Colossians 1:28-29).

9. Biblical Counseling depends on the sufficiency of Scripture instead of the traditions and theories of man (Colossians 2:8-9, 2Timohty 3:16-17, Psalm 1:1-2, Psalm 19:7-11).

10. Biblical Counseling is rooted and grounded in a worldview that all things are from God, through God, and to God; Therefore all things must be evaluated from His perspective (Romans 11:36). Questions such as the following are addressed through God and His Word.

    a. What is the nature of man, and what is his relationship to God?
    b. What is man's fundamental problem?
    c. How should we and how do we relate to our fellow human beings?
    d. What values should guide, and what values do guide our attitudes and actions?
    e. How can man solve his basic problems?
    f. What specific changes should he make?
    g. Who/what is the agent for such change?
    h. What are the goals of these changes?

11. True Biblical Counseling will demonstrate:

    a. A high view of God in His Character, Nature, Attributes, etc.
    b. A high view of the Sufficiency of Scripture.
    c. An accurate anthropology (man is basically evil and in need of salvation/sanctification).
    d. A Biblical understanding of the purpose of the Church.
    e. A Biblical view of Church Leadership.
    f. Insight that is based on Biblical foundations.

g. Methodologies that are based on Biblical foundations.
   h. Goals that are God-centered instead of man centered.

(Concept #11 adapted from Lance Quinn Senior Pastor of Little Rock Bible Church)

So Why Promote Biblical Counseling Above The Others?

Key Point: The Bible gives us all we need for mental soundness and for understanding and dealing with the basic needs of the inner, immaterial man. God's Word instructs us to find from Scripture alone our principles for living, our understanding of human attitudes, motives, behaviors, and our solutions for man's, non-organic, immaterial, inner problems and what the world calls psychological problems.

1. Scripture warns us not to trust human wisdom for principles for living, understanding of human attitudes, motives, behaviors, and our solution for man's inner problems—problems that are non-organic in nature (Psalm 1:1-2 and Colossians 2:8).

2. Scripture warns us not to trust our own wisdom because we can be deceived by our own wisdom (Proverbs 3:5-6; 14:12; 16:2, 25; 21:2, and Jeremiah 17:9).

3. Scripture instructs us that God's wisdom is superior to man's wisdom. Therefore, man's wisdom should not be added to God's wisdom as solutions to man's inner problems—Problems that are non-organic in nature (1 Corinthians 1:21, 25; 2:2-5, 3:20, and Isaiah 55:8-11).

4. Scripture instructs us that God's wisdom is sufficient to counsel the inner Person—the immaterial aspect of man (Psalm 119:24, 99, 100, Hebrews 4:12, and Psalm 19:7-11).

(Insights from the section adapted from The Heart of Man and the Mental Disorders by Rich Thomson)

Why Is It Futile To Mix Human Wisdom With The Bible?

Key Point: The idea of integrating human wisdom with the Bible in counseling the inner man is contradictory to Scripture. The reasons given for integrating human wisdom with the Bible are contradictory to Scripture as well.

1. **Reason A:** We should integrate because Scripture shows that man should gain insight on his inner self by observation.

   Response: On the contrary, God's Word warns man not to trust in his own insight about himself concerning his inner man. When Scripture acknowledges man's observation about himself as true, it is simply saying that man's observation must be included in the Bible in order for man to know that the observations are true. See Psalm 1:1-2, Colossians 2:8,

Proverbs 3:5-6; 14:12; 16:25; 24:30-34, Jeremiah 17:9, Isaiah 55:8-11, 1 Corinthians 15:33 (written by Menander, but confirmed as true by Scripture), Acts 17:28 (written by a Greek poet, but confirmed as true by Scripture), Titus 1:12-13 (quote from a pagan prophet that is confirmed as true by Scripture).

2. **Reason B:** We should integrate because "all truth is God's truth."

   Response: Scripture says that man can easily deceive himself and should not trust his own assessments. He needs truth revealed from the One who knows all truth in order to be sure man's "truth" is actually truth. (John 14:26; 16:13; 17:17, Proverbs 3:5-6, 2 Corinthians 12:12, Hebrews 2:3-4, and Mark 16: 17-20)

3. **Reason C:** We should integrate because human observations are general revelation from God, which supplement His special revelation in the Bible.

   Response: This is a misrepresentation of general revelation. God's word describes general revelation as revelation about God (not specifically about man), which is given to mankind in general through nature, providence, and conscience. As such, all of God's general revelation to mankind is also revealed through His special revelation in the Bible plus much, much more (Psalm 19:1-6, Romans 1:18-20; 2:14-15, and Acts 14:17; Basic Theology, Ryrie, pp. 28, 33 and The Moody Handbook of Theology, 1993, pp.186-87)

4. **Reason D:** We should integrate because just as it is acceptable to rely upon an unbelieving plumber or surgeon or auto mechanic, it is acceptable to receive counsel from human wisdom concerning the problems in our lives.

   Response: Plumbing, surgery and autos are physical things not spiritual things. God's Word tells believers not to rely upon the wisdom of man to meet the inner problems of their lives. Christians are not promised perfect physical health or perfect plumbing, but they are promised perfect peace (Psalm 1:1-2, Colossians 2:8, Proverbs 3:5-6, and Isaiah 26:3).

5. **Reason E:** We should integrate because we are to "spoil the Egyptians" as Israel did by taking the best of human wisdom and leaving the rest.

   Response: Scripture says that Israel took the physical gold, silver, and jewels, not the philosophy of life from the Egyptians. God was seeking to change their philosophy. Believers are not to take the philosophy of life that comes from the world (Psalm 1:1-2 and Colossians 2:8).

6. **Reason F:** We should integrate because there are some people who can only grow spiritually if human wisdom removes the barriers to growth within them.

   Response: If this is true it implies that Scripture is insufficient to help one grow. It also implies that we need human wisdom *and* the Scripture in order to help one grow. God's Word says, however, that spiritual growth depends entirely upon a person's relationship with

Him and His Word, not upon human wisdom. Human wisdom denies sin as the problem and places responsibility on outside uncontrollable responses (2 Timothy 3:16-17, 2 Peter 3:18, James 1:2-4, Ephesians 4:15, 1 Timothy 1:5, 1 Peter 2:2, and 2 Peter 1:5-8).

(Insights from the section adapted from <u>The Heart of Man and the Mental Disorders</u> by Rich Thomson)

Key Point: *If we assume that it is necessary to integrate human wisdom and the Bible, we give rise to logical conclusions which are contradicted by the Scripture.*

1. **Reason A**: If integration is necessary, the logical conclusion is that God has made us to depend upon human wisdom in addition to His wisdom for our inner lives.

    Response: God's Word says that we should depend upon His wisdom alone. The basic systems of psychology are developed by unbelievers. We should neither listen to nor be held captive by it (Psalm 1:1-3, Colossians 2:8, Proverbs 3:5-6; 14:12; 16:25).

2. **Reason B:** If integration is necessary, then the logical conclusion is that the apostles and prophets were somehow handicapped in their inner persons since we have much greater knowledge than they had concerning the inner self.

    Response: The Apostles and Prophets had all they needed for their inner persons (Philippians 4:11-13, Hebrews 11:32-37, 1Corinthians 2:1-5, 2 Corinthians 12:9-10, Acts 7:54-60, and 2 Timothy 3:16-17).

3. **Reason C:** If integration is necessary, then the logical conclusion is that the fruit of the Spirit is not enough for meeting the trials and challenges of life.

    Response: The Holy Spirit is enough, but we don't walk enough in the Holy Spirit (1Corinthians 10:13, Proverbs 18:4, 2 Timothy 3:16-17, 2Corinthians 4:7-9, and Galatians 5:22-23)

(Insights from section adapted from <u>The Heart of Man and The Mental Disorders</u> by Rich Thomson)

Qualifications of a Biblical Counselor

1. A biblical counselor should be one who is guarded and governed by the Holy Spirit thus displaying the fruits of the Holy Spirit in attitudes, values, words and actions (Galatians 6:1).

2. A biblical Counselor should be one who is aware and honest about his own sinful tendencies and character flaws seeking to deal with them accordingly (Galatians 6:1).

3. A biblical counselor should be one who ministers by the Word of God and does not use any theories or practices that contradict or violate God's standards (2Timothy 4:1-5).

4. A biblical counselor should be one who seeks to help others recover from the consequences of poor decisions (Galatians 6:2).

5. A biblical counselor should be one who seeks to help others confess and repent of sin (Galatians 6:1-2).

6. A biblical counselor should be one who seeks to help others function in spiritual maturity in all aspects of life (Ephesians 4:11-16).

7. A biblical counselor should be one who seeks to hold others accountable to stay away from people, places, and products that will lead them into sin (Hebrews 3:12-13).

8. A biblical counselor should be one who seeks to stimulate others to love and good deeds (Hebrews 10:19-25).

9. A biblical counselor should be one who is not quarrelsome but kind to all (2Timothy 2:24).

10. A biblical counselor should be one who is able to teach others the Truth of God's Word (2Timohty 2:24).

11. A biblical counselor should be one who is able to practice patience when others are mistreating him (2Timohty 2:24).

12. A biblical counselor should be one who is able to gently correct those who are in opposition to the Truth (2Timothy 2:25).

13. A biblical counselor should be one who builds up others with his words (Ephesians 4:29).

Section Two
The Theological Foundations for Biblical Counseling

Key point: Christians must develop in biblical theology in order to provide genuine biblical counseling. Biblical theology can be defined as the systematic understanding of what the Scriptures say about various topics. This insight is gained from the proper exegesis of Scripture and classified accordingly. We cannot lead people into godly beliefs, values, attitudes, relationships and behavior without developing a biblical theology. There are several key doctrines of the Christian faith that come out of proper exegesis of Scripture and are classified accordingly. These doctrines are foundational to biblical theology and essential for the principles and practice of genuine biblical counseling. The ascertaining and application of these essential doctrines will lead to God-honoring biblical counseling. Deficiency in the ascertaining and practice of these doctrines result in bad theology and unbiblical counseling. (For more on this read A Theology of Christian Counseling by Jay Adams.)

I. A biblical counselor can provide insight into Who the Creator is, how He operates, and what He expects of us as the counselor understands and develops in the Doctrine of God.

    A. Biblical counselors need to learn the Person of God (Trinity).
    B. Biblical counselors need to learn the Character of God.
    C. Biblical counselors need to learn the Will of God.
    D. Biblical counselors need to learn the Work of God.
    E. Biblical counselors need to learn the arguments to prove the existence of God.

II. A biblical counselor can provide relevant, real, and accurate insight into the issues of life as the counselor understands and develops in the Doctrine of Bible.

    A. Biblical counselors need to learn the nature and history of the Bible.
    B. Biblical counselors need to learn the divisions of the Bible.
    C. Biblical counselors need to learn the main idea of the Bible.
    D. Biblical counselors need to learn how to prove the sufficiency of the Bible.
    E. Biblical counselors need to learn how to prove the inerrancy of the Bible.

III. A biblical counselor can lead people to understand who is the source of their existence, who should be the Prophet, Priest, and King of their Life, who can bring the ultimate satisfaction of their life and who is the solution to their problems, as the counselor understands and develops in the Doctrine of Jesus Christ.

   A. Biblical counselors need to learn the Peron of Jesus Christ.
   B. Biblical counselors need to learn the Nature of Jesus Christ.
   C. Biblical counselors need to learn the Work of Jesus Christ.
   D. Biblical counselors need to learn the Will of Jesus Christ.
   E. Biblical counselors need to learn the Offices of Jesus Christ.

IV. A biblical counselor can provide insight into the One who will convict, equip, guide, empower, and transform people into a life that is productive and pleasing to God as the counselor understands and develops in the Doctrine of the Holy Spirit.

   A. Biblical counselors need to learn the Peron of the Holy Spirit.
   B. Biblical counselors need to learn the Nature of the Holy Spirit.
   C. Biblical counselors need to learn the Work of the Holy Spirit.
   D. Biblical counselors need to learn the Will of the Holy Spirit.
   E. Biblical counselors need to learn the Offices of the Holy Spirit.

V. A biblical counselor can help individuals understand why mankind operates and acts the way they do as the counselor understands and develops in the Doctrine of Man.

   A. Biblical counselors need to learn the nature of man.
   B. Biblical counselors need to learn the problem of man.
   C. Biblical counselors need to learn the purpose of the creation of man.
   D. Biblical counselors need to learn God's solutions to man's problem.
   E. Biblical counselors need to learn the process of spiritual growth.

VI. A biblical counselor can explain the reality of corruption and evil, and how to deal with it properly as the counselor understands and develops in the Doctrine of Sin.

   A. Biblical counselors need to learn the nature of sin.
   B. Biblical counselors need to learn the effects of sin.
   C. Biblical counselors need to learn the power of sin.
   D. Biblical counselors need to learn the origin of sin.
   E. Biblical counselors need to learn how to deal with sin.

VII. **A biblical counselor can lead people into understanding what true deliverance looks like and how to obtain it as the counselor understands and develops in the Doctrine of Salvation.**

    A. Biblical counselors need to learn the components of salvation.
    B. Biblical counselors need to learn the origin of salvation.
    C. Biblical counselors need to learn the way to salvation.
    D. Biblical counselors need to learn how to give the message of salvation.
    E. Biblical counselors need to learn how to rebuke false messages of salvation.

VIII. **A biblical counselor can provide insight into the accurate meaning of community and how to connect, gives, serve, and be served in it as the counselor understands and develops in the Doctrine of the Church.**

    A. Biblical counselors need to learn the purpose of the Church.
    B. Biblical counselors need to learn the objectives of the Church.
    C. Biblical counselors need to learn the practice of the Church.
    D. Biblical counselors need to learn the structure of the Church.
    E. BiBblical counselors need to learn the various dominations of the Church.

IX. **A biblical counselor can help individuals develop hope in the future as the counselor understands and develops in the Doctrine of Last Things.**

    A. Biblical counselors need to learn about the rapture.
    B. Biblical counselors need to learn about tribulation period.
    C. Biblical counselors need to learn about the thousand year reign of Jesus Christ.
    D. Biblical counselors need to learn about the work of Satan and Demons during tribulation, and thousand year reign period.
    E. Biblical counselors need to learn the various views in relation to the doctrine of last things.

X. **A biblical counselor can help individuals understand their divine help and their divine hindrances as the counselor understands and develops in the Doctrine of Angels and Demons.**

    A. Biblical counselors need to learn the Nature of Angels.
    B. Biblical counselors need to learn the Work of Angels.
    C. Biblical counselors need to learn the Nature of Demons.
    D. Biblical counselors need to learn the Work of Demons.
    E. Biblical counselors need to learn the Offices of Angels and Demons.

XI. A biblical counselor can guide individuals into where they should lead and should follow as the counselor understands and develops in the doctrine of Leadership.

A. Biblical counselors need to learn the purpose of leadership.
B. Biblical counselors need to learn the practice of leadership.
C. Biblical counselors need to learn the problems of leadership.
D. Biblical counselors need to learn the various types of leadership.
E. Biblical counselors need to learn the proper response to leadership.

XII. A biblical counselor can help individuals learn how to operate in the good works they were created to walk in as the counselor understands and develops in the Doctrine of Spiritual Gifts.

A. Biblical counselors need to learn the definition of spiritual gifts.
B. Biblical counselors need to learn the purpose of spiritual gifts.
C. Biblical counselors need to learn the mentor gifts.
D. Biblical counselors need to learn the ministry gifts.
E. Biblical counselors need to learn the manifestation gifts.

XIII. A biblical counselor can direct individuals in the point and practice of putting off sin and putting on right living as the counselor understands and develops in the Doctrine of Sanctification.

A. Biblical counselors need to learn the definition of sanctification.
B. Biblical counselors need to learn the purpose of sanctification.
C. Biblical counselors need to learn the stages of sanctification.
D. Biblical counselors need to learn the work of God in sanctification.
E. Biblical counselors need to learn how man should operate in sanctification.

XIV. A biblical counselor can provide guidance into managing life and resources as the counselor understands and develops in the Doctrine of Stewardship.

A. Biblical counselors need to learn the definition of stewardship.
B. Biblical counselors need to learn the stewardship of time.
C. Biblical counselors need to learn the stewardship of money.
D. Biblical counselors need to learn the stewardship of talents.
E. Biblical counselors need to learn the stewardship of relationships.

XV. **A biblical counselor can challenge people to anticipate the judgment and rewards of obedient and disobedient living to come as the counselor understands and develops in the Doctrine of Judgment and Rewards.**

    A. Biblical counselors need to learn the definition of Bema Judgment and the White Throne Judgment.
    B. Biblical counselors need to learn why people will be judged.
    C. Biblical counselors need to learn the rewards Christians can gain.
    D. Biblical counselors need to learn the rewards Christians can lose.
    E. Biblical counselors need to learn what will be judged.

XVI. **A biblical counselor can help individuals connect with God as the counselor understands and develops in the Disciplines of the Christian faith.**

    A. Biblical counselors need to learn the purpose and practice of confessing sin.
    B. Biblical counselors need to learn the purpose and practice of repenting of sin.
    C. Biblical counselors need to learn the purpose and practice of meditating on the Word of God.
    D. Biblical counselors need to learn the purpose and practice of forgiving others as God has prescribed.
    E. Biblical counselors need to learn the purpose and practice of living the truth.
    F. Biblical counselors need to learn the purpose and practice of serving others according to one's spiritual gifts.
    G. Biblical counselors need to learn the purpose and practice of praying and worshipping.

XVII. **A biblical counselor can help individuals connect with each other as the counselor understands and develops in the Duties of the Christian Faith.**

    A. Biblical counselors need to learn the purpose and practice of bearing burdens of fellow Christians.
    B. Biblical counselors need to learn the purpose and practice of meeting needs of fellow Christians.
    C. Biblical counselors need to learn the purpose and practice of proclaiming the Gospel to unbelievers.
    D. Biblical counselors need to learn the purpose and practice of defending the Gospel to unbelievers.
    E. Biblical counselors need to learn the purpose and practice of giving finically to support the work and workers of the Church.
    F. Biblical counselors need to learn the purpose and practice of corporate fellowshipping with fellow Christians.
    G. Biblical counselors need to learn the purpose and practice of corporate praying and worshipping with fellow Christians.

XVIII. **A biblical counselor can help individuals function as God wills according to their role in life as the counselor develops in his/her understanding of the Demographics of the Christian Faith.**

    A. Biblical counselors need to know and understand the practice of being a godly man.
    B. Biblical counselors need to know and understand the practice of being a godly woman.
    C. Biblical counselors need to know and understand the practice of being a godly husband.
    D. Biblical counselors need to know and understand the practice of being a godly wife.
    E. Biblical counselors need to know and understand the practice of being a godly senior citizen.
    F. Biblical counselors need to know and understand the practice of being a godly young adult.
    G. Biblical counselors need to know and understand the practice of being a godly teenager.
    H. Biblical counselors need to know and understand the practice of being a godly child.

Section Three
Who is God?

Key Point: God is man's environment. He is creator and controller of all. There is no escaping God. Anyone who does not line up with God will be out of harmony with their environment. Counsel that is not God-centered is evil and thus out of harmony with God leading to more corruption, chaos, and confusion in life. There must be a promotion of God's Character, will, and ways as revealed in Scripture in counseling or one will not find genuine hope and solutions for their problems. Any counseling system that does not represent and submit to the character, will, and ways of God is in competition with God and is at odds with God's design. We were created to know God, to become like God in the essence of our character, and to be useful to God in our existence. Therefore, it is imperative for us to develop a proper view of God. (For more on this, read A Theology of Christian Counseling by Jay Adams.)

I. **What is a description of God? (See 1Timothy 1:17, Romans 11:36, and Act 17:24-26.)**
   A. Lord of all who made the world and all things in it.
   B. The Lord of heaven and earth who does not dwell in temples made with hands.
   C. The invisible, immortal, eternal King who created and controls all that exist and has existed. All things are from Him, through Him and to Him.
   D. The only true Lord of heaven and earth who gives to all people life and breath and all things, as well as, controls life and death.

II. **How can we prove that God exists? (See Romans 1:18-20, 1:28-32, 2:14-15.)**
   A. Cosmological proof: Every known thing in the universe has a cause. The universe itself had to have a cause. Non-life cannot produce life. Whoever created life and the universe had to be greater than the life and universe it created. The only logical conclusion is that it had to be God who is the ultimate cause of life and existence.
   B. Teleological proof: The universe and humans were designed with purpose and order. There had to be some being larger than the life and the universe with intelligence, purpose and power to create human beings and the universe with such order, purpose and design. The creator had to be God.

C. Moral proof: Man has a sense of right and wrong. This reality of right and wrong is universal. Man's desire for justice is universal. This idea of right and wrong and justice had to come from a source greater than man. This source had to be God who created man and the world with purpose, order and morality.
D. These proofs seek to show that the universe has God as its cause. This God has purpose, power, intelligence, and order as reflected in His creation. This God has a sense of right and wrong and justice, which is reflected in man's innate understanding of right, wrong, and justice.

III. What are some key Characteristics of God? (See Psalm 40:5, 48:1, 95:3-5.)
A. Omnipotent: God has the power to do everything He desires. No one can stop His will. He posses all power and authority. God is able to do everything consistent with His Character and nature. He has power and control over everything that exists. God's power is unlimited. No one has the ability to match God's power (see Isaiah 14:27, Ecclesiastes 7:13-14, Lamentations 3:37, Colossians 1:17, and 1Chronicles 29:11-13).
B. Omniscience: God knows Himself, all people and all things perfectly and precisely. He knows everything possible, actual and imaginable all at once. God does not need any new knowledge because He knows all things (see Romans 11:33, Psalm 139:1-6, Psalm 147:5, and 1John 3:20).
C. Omnipresence: God does not have size or spatial dimensions. He is present at every point of space with His whole being. He is everywhere at all times. (Systematic Theology by Wayne Grudem pp.168-169.) (See Jeremiah 23:23-24, Psalm 139:7-10, and 1Kings 8:27.)
D. Spirit: God exists as a being that is not made of matter. God has no parts or dimensions. He is unable to be perceived by our bodily senses and is more excellent than any other kind of existence (Systematic Theology by Wayne Grudem pp.187-188). (See John 4:24, John 1:18 and 1Timothy 1:17.)
E. Eternal: God has no beginning and end. He never began to exist. He has always been. He has never started or stopped being God (see Psalm 90:2, Job 36:26, and Exodus 3:14).
F. Transcendent: God is distinct from His creation. He is greater than the creation and He is independent of the creation. He is not subject to the limitations of humanity and the universe (Systematic Theology by Wayne Grudem pp. 267). (See Acts 17:24-32, and Ephesians 4:6.)
G. Immanent: God is involved in His creation for it is continually dependent on Him for its existence and functioning. He is interested and very much involved in the governing and guiding of His creation. He interacts with us. He seeks to relate with us (see Acts 17:24-32 and Ephesians 4:6).

H. Good: God is right and benevolent in what He does. He does what is of the highest standard of what could be defined as proper. He does what will benefit mankind (Luke 18:19, Psalm 119:68, James 1:17, Psalm 145:9).

I. Triune: There is only One God. This one God eternally exists as three distinct persons: Father, Son, and Holy Spirit and each person is fully God (see Deuteronomy 6:4-5, Genesis 1:26, Genesis 11:1-7, and Matthew 28:19).

IV. How much of God can we truly know?

A. Through creation and our conscience we come to learn that God exists (see Romans 1:18-20, and Psalm 19:1-6).

B. Through salvation we come into a relationship with Him that moves beyond intellectual knowledge about Him (see John 6:26-40, 10:27-29, and Romans 8:16-17).

C. Through obedience to God we come to learn God's character experientially to the fullness of our finiteness (see John 8:31-32, 14:21 and Ephesians 3:14-21).

V. How Does God Operate in this World?

A. God operates in the world through His providence—God cares for and controls the entire universe through natural and supernatural means (see Colossians 1:17, Ecclesiastes 7:13-14, and Psalm 145).

B. God operates in the world through His people—God uses the Body of Christ on earth to evangelize and disciple people for His Kingdom (see 2Corinthains 5:18-20, Ephesians 4:11-17, and Matthew 28:18-20).

C. God operates in the world through His precepts – God uses His Word/ Scriptures to guide us into the way we are to relate with God, others, ourselves, the world and even our circumstances (see Psalm 19:7-11, Proverbs 30:5-6, Isaiah 55:6-11, and Psalm 119:1-16).

VI. What is God's Objective in the World?

A. God's objective is to make the greatness of His Character known throughout the entire world (see Isaiah 48:11 and Romans 11:36).

B. The greatness of God's character is seen in His salvation of people from all nationalities from the penalty, power, and presence of sin unto a right relationship with Himself resulting in his people showing forth His character through their service (see Ephesians 2:1-10 and 1Peter 4:11).

C. The greatness of God's character is seen in the transformation of all the people He saves into His Image to be with Him forever as He reigns in Heaven and on Earth (see 1John 3:1-3, Colossians 3:1-4, Titus 2:11-14, and Revelation 21:1-3).

VII. What Do You Believe about God?

A. What we believe about God is revealed in how we live (Galatians 6:7-8).
B. The wrong ideas about God lead to a life of corruption (Galatians 6:7-8).
C. The right view of God can lead to Eternal Life (Knowing God intimately) (Galatians 6:7-8, John 17:3).
D. The wrong ideas about God will lead us to do our own thing and we will get upset with God when we suffer the consequences of our disobedience (Proverbs 19:2-3).
E. The right view of God can lead us to fear (show reverence and respect) Him and His standards and turn away from a lifestyle of selfishness and evil living (Proverbs 1:7,8:13,9:10).
F. The wrong ideas about God will lead us to compare ourselves and situations to others and believe God is unfair for letting our situation stand as it is (Psalm 73).
G. The right view of God can lead us to accept what He allows whether good or bad while submitting to what He says knowing we will one day have to give an account of our lives to God. (Ecclesiastes 7:13-14, 12:13-14).

VIII. Gaining a Fresh Perspective on God

A. What comes to mind when we think of God is the most important thing about us (Matthew 16:13-17).
B. As foundation is to the temple so an accurate view of God is to worship (John 4:21-24).
C. The essence of idolatry is to imagine things about God that are not true and to act is if they are true (James 1:13-17).
D. Left to ourselves we tend to reduce God to personal concepts that give us a sense of security and control (Exodus 32:1-14).
E. Sin has led us to believe that God exists for us instead of the reality that we exist for God. This logic leads us to measure if God is for us or against us by how well He solves our problems, eases our pain, or provides some form of blessing we treasure (Psalm 73).
F. Since we exist to Glorify God (to show the Greatness of His Character) and God does not exist to glorify us we must reevaluate our priorities (Isaiah 43:6-7).
G. God did not save us from the penalty of sin, the power of sin and soon the presence of sin so we could make much of ourselves; God saved us so that we would make much of Him (1Peter 2:9, Romans 6:1-23,7:4, Ephesians 1:3-6).
H. God has chosen us to manifest His Glory yet is seems we have chosen Him to satisfy our personal matters and ambitions (1Peter 2:9, John 6:26-27).
I. God's Glory is the ultimate objective of all things; Our lives should not be examined by how much God has done for us but by how much Glory God has received through us (Romans 11:36, 1Corinthians 10:31, Colossians 3:17, 23).
J. We matter much to God but what matters most is His Glory; a perfect God must value what is of supreme value or He's not perfect. If people mattered more than His Glory

then we would be objects of worship and not Him; That would make us higher than God and God less than us (Ezekiel 36:22-37).

K. The central issue in life is not what kind of obedience will get God to make our lives more manageable and successful; The central issue in life is what kind of obedience will make God's Character more visible (Matthew 5:14-16).

L. God's highest agenda for our lives is not that we live good moral lives; God's highest agenda for our lives is that our good moral lives reflect His Glory (1Corinthians 10:31).

*(Notes taken from **The Knowledge of the Holy** by A.W. Tozer, **Experiencing Christ Within** by Dwight Edwards and **God's Passion for His Glory** by John Piper)*

IX. The Premise of Trusting God (Proverbs 3:5)

A. Trusting God means to rely on and place confidence in who He is.
B. Trusting God must start from the inside out.
C. We must trust that God is:
 1. Sovereign – controls all things at all times for His Glory and our good (Lamentations. 3:37-38, Ephesians 1:11, 1Timothy 6:13-16).
 2. Infinite in wisdom – knows the best course of action and the way to bring about the best results (Colossians 2:1-3, Romans 11:33).
 3. Perfect in love – seeks the highest good of individuals (Psalm 32:10, 1John 4:9-10, Lamentations 3:22-23).

X. The Pitfall to Trusting God (Proverbs 3:5)

A. The pitfall to trusting God is relying on your own insight. Relying on your own insight is having a human observation apart from a biblical interpretation (Psalm 73).
B. Relying on your own insight alone leads to self deception, self protection, self centeredness, and self promotion (Proverbs 14:12).
C. Signs of leaning on your own understanding:
 1. Inflexible / your way or no way in almost every aspect of life
 2. Preoccupied with making things happens to you, for you, through you as you desire instead of submission to the Power, Presence, Provision of God as He as ordained and allowed.
 3. Thoughts, words, actions are predicated on the response of people/ outcome of events not the will of God.
 4. Thinking/speaking/living as if the outcome of your life depends on you.

XI. The Process of Trusting God (Proverbs 3:6)

A. We must acknowledge God in every aspect of life.

B. To acknowledge God means to acquire God's instruction for every aspect of life (Matthew 6:33).

C. To acknowledge God means to obey God's instruction in every aspect of life (Matthew 7:24-27).

XII. The Promise of Trusting God (Proverbs 3:6)

A. God promised to make our way of life straight if we acknowledge Him.

B. To make our way straight means to make us morally upright, productive and satisfied (Psalm 37:6, John 15:1-5, Matthew 5:6).

C. God did not promise freedom from failure, freedom from trials, freedom from problems; nor did He promise material riches, or realization of all our expectations (Ecclesiastes 7:14, 20, John 16:33, Proverbs 13:12).

What Happens when You Live as if God is Not Enough?
Self-Centered
(Psalm 10:3-4)

You live as if all things are for you (God is nonexistent)
You live as if all things are about you (God is nonexistent)
You live as if everything revolves around you (God is nonexistent)

Self-Ambitious
(James 3:13-16)

You become preoccupied with what you want in place of obedience to God

I want….
I need…
I demand……
I must have…..
I can't do without….

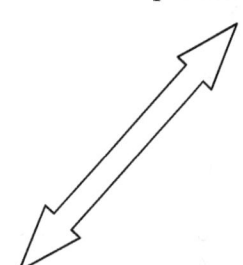   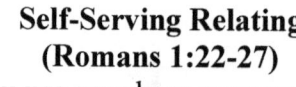

Self-Serving
(Philippians 3:17-19)
You become consumed with the pleasures of this life

Self-Serving Relating
(Romans 1:22-27)
You use people as avenues for your satisfaction

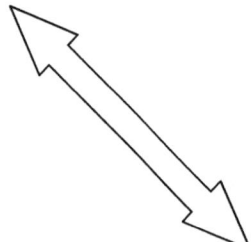   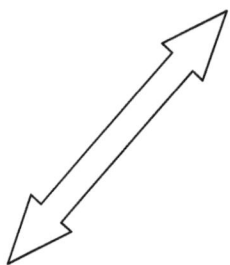

Anger
(Numbers 20:1-13, Proverb 19:2-3)

You get upset with People and God when they don't come through as you want

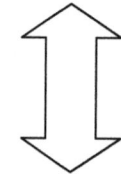

Despair
(Ecclesiastes 2:17)

Sorrow with no hope because you live life without considering the will and ways of God

(Idea Adapted from Jim Berg)

What Happens When You Trust God with Your Life?

Belief
(Psalm 73:25-26)

You accept the truth that God is doing enough
You accept the truth that God is enough

Contentment
(Philippians 4:10-14)

You accept what you have
You accept what God
   has allowed in your life
You accept who you have
You learn to live without when
   necessary

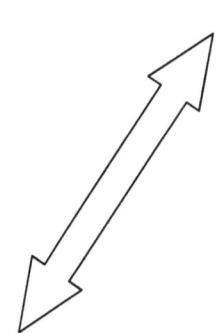

Thanksgiving
(1Thessalonians 5:18)
You appreciate that God is in Control
You appreciate that God will work all things
   to your Good

Submission
(Romans 12:1-3
You obey God
You follow God

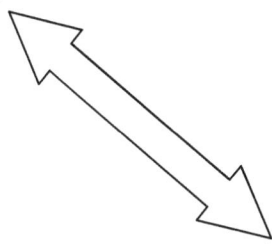

Hope
(Romans 5:1-5)

You put your expectation in what God will do according to His Promises

(Idea adapted from Jim Berg)

Questions to Consider

1. What do you tend to believe about God as it relates to your life?
   _____
   _____

2. How have you come to that conclusion? Please explain.
   _____
   _____

3. What seems to matter most to you, God's Glory or your personal matters and ambitions? Please explain.
   _____
   _____

4. How do your attitudes, words, actions, and relationship patterns reflect your answer in question 3? Please explain.
   _____
   _____

5. What do you need to change about your perspective of God?
   _____
   _____

6. How will changing your perspective of God impact your view of your present situation or circumstances? Please explain.
   _____
   _____

7. How will changing your perspective of God impact your relationship with God?
   _____
   _____

8. How will changing your perspective of God impact your relationship with others?
   _____
   _____

9. What is the premise of trusting God?
   _____
   _____

10. What is the pitfall to trusting God?
    _____
    _____

11. What are the signs of leaning on your own understanding?
    _____
    _____

12. What is the process of trusting God?
    _____
    _____

13. What is the promise of trusting God?
    _____
    _____

14. How are you trusting God right now?
    _____
    _____

Practical Tools for Embracing God and Meditating on Who He Is

There are few characteristics of God on the following page. They are placed under the far left column called Characteristics of God to embrace. Immediately to the right of the column of Characteristics of God to embrace are application assignments columns that correspond to the Characteristics of God to embrace column. They are labeled, The Perspective we should have as a result of embracing this characteristic, The Practice we should develop as a result of embracing this characteristic, The Patterns of Relating we should have as a result of embracing this characteristic. Along with that chart is another chart of documentation according to how you embrace those characteristics accordingly. In addition, is a chart given of more characteristics and assignment to follow.

Step 1 (*Characteristic of God to Embrace*)
As you find the particular characteristic of God you want to embrace under the column labeled "Characteristic of God to Embrace" Read the definition of that characteristic and read the Bible verse placed with that definition. Place this information on index card that you can take with you daily. Put the Characteristic and the definition on one side of the card and then place the verse written out on the other side of the card. Review the card three times a day. In the morning, in the noon day and at night

Step 2 (The Perspective we should have as a result of embracing this characteristic)
Along with that characteristic of God you want to embrace review the application assignment under the column "The Perspective we should have as a result of embracing this characteristic" that corresponds to the characteristic you are seeking to embrace. Read the perspective and read the Bible verse placed with that perspective. Place this information on an index card that you can take with you daily. Put the perspective on one side of the card and then place the verse written out on the other side of the card. Review the card 30 times a day. All throughout the day.

Step 3 (The Practice we should develop as a result of embracing this characteristic)
Along with reviewing the application assignment under "The Perspective we should have as a result of embracing this characteristic" column, you want to review the application assignment under the column "The Practice we should develop as a result of embracing this characteristic" that corresponds to the characteristic you are seeking to embrace. Read the practice and read the Bible verse placed with that perspective. Place this information on an index card that you can take with you daily. Identify ways you can apply that practice during the week. As you apply that practice review that index card.

Step 4 (The Patterns of Relating we should walk in as a result of embracing this characteristic)

Along with reviewing the application assignment under "The Practice we should develop as result have as a result of embracing this characteristic", you want to review the application assignment under the column "The Patterns of Relating we should walk in as result of embracing this characteristic" that corresponds to the characteristic you are seeking to embrace. Read the pattern and read the Bible verse placed with that pattern. Place this information on an index card that you can take with you daily. Identify ways you can apply that pattern of relating during the week. As you apply pattern of relating review that index card.

Step 5(Documentation)

As you walk through the practice of step 1 – step 4 document this information on the chart that follows the chart of characteristics accordingly.

Characteristics of God to embrace	The Perspective We Should have as a result of embracing this Characteristic?	The Practice we should develop as result of embracing this Characteristic?	The Patterns of relating we should walk in as a result of embracing this Characteristic
Supreme – He is first and foremost before all things; all created things were designed to reflect the greatness of God; His glory is our goal. (Colossians 1:15-19)	I exist for His glory (Romans 11:36}	Live for the audience of God alone, Put God first (1Corinthians 10:31)	Consider God's Glory not your personal gain when relating to others (Philippians 2:1-4)
Sovereign - God controls all things; nothing happens unless God allows it or ordains it; He upholds all things by His power (Ecclesiastes 7:13-14)	My life is in the hands of God and He has it under control (Ecclesiastes 9:1)	Trust God with all your heart by focusing on what you are called to do and stop trying to play God with your circumstances (Proverbs 3: 5-8)	Stop trying to control what others think, say, and do in relation to you or with anything and accept your role under God with them (Matthew 22:34-40)
Sufficient – God is enough and He is doing enough in relation to my life (Psalm 145:17-21)	God is enough and He is doing enough for me (Psalm 73:25-28)	Enjoy what God provides without complaining about what you do not have (Philippians 4:10-14)	Give to others knowing God will supply your needs (Luke 6:30-36)
Holy – unique and set apart from sin while dedicated to His glory (Isaiah 6:1-4)	I must be in the world but be set apart for Christ (1Peter 1:13-16)	Present your body as a living and holy sacrifice to God (Romans 12:1)	Treat others as precious and valuable to God (1Thessalonians 4:1-8)
Loving – seeks the highest good of others; gives himself for the good of others; gives himself to be a blessing to others (Romans 5:8-11)	God is always looking out for me no matter what happens (Hebrews 13:5-6)	Live to be blessing to God (1Corinthians 10:31)	Bear burdens and meet needs of others (Galatians 6:1-2, Titus 3:14)
Wise – He knows and works the best course of action to bring about His greatest glory and our greatest good (Job 9:4-12)	God knows how to bring about the best results for my life (Romans 8:28-39)	Listen to God and follow Him accordingly (Ecclesiastes 5:1-2)	Listen to others with the intent to learn what to do or what not to do accordingly (Proverbs 18:15)
Gracious – showing favor, being a benefit and being generous to people who deserve punishment without them having to earn it or work for it (Ephesians 2:8-10)	I will receive blessings that I don't deserve because of my relationship with God (Psalm 103:1-8)	Give thanks to God and enjoy what He provides (1Thessaloninas 5:18)	Be kind and beneficial to people who don't deserve it (Luke 6:30-36)
Merciful – not giving people the punishment they deserve (2Samuel 24:14-25)	God is always cutting me slack (Psalm 103:9-10)	Repent of all known sin accordingly to God (2Corinthians 7:10-11)	Cut people some slack without dismissing their sin (Romans 12:17-18)
Forgiving – canceled the debt owed by sin; will not hold sin against us (Psalm 103:1-14)	God will always forgive if I ask for it (1John 1:9)	Confess sins to God accordingly (Psalm 32:1-5)	Forgive others as you have been forgiven by God (Matthew 18:21-35)
Faithful – God will always be true to His Word; He will always do whatever He says or promises (Numbers 23:19)	The Lord will never leave me nor forsake me He will always be there (Hebrews 13:5-6)	Serve God faithfully while continuing to wait on His return (1Corinthians 15:58)	Be faithful to others according to the level of the relationship (Proverbs 27:6)

What Characteristic of God will you embrace today?	How did this characteristic of God impact you perspective of life today?	How did this characteristic of God impact the way you lived life today?	How did this characteristic of God impact the way you related to others today?
Day 1			
Day 2			
Day 3			
Day 4			
Day 5			
Day 6			
Day 7			
Day 8			
Day 9			
Day 10			

Section Four
THE DOCTRINE OF CHRIST

Key Point: There is no deliverance from the evil, pain, suffering, problems, sin or sickness without understanding and embracing the Deliver Jesus Christ. Jesus Christ is the grace that has appeared to all men and is the provider of grace to all men. Embracing who He is and what He has done is essential for life transformation. Biblical Counseling is the tool by which one is led to the Deliver and His deliverance. There is no biblical counseling without embracing the Person and work of Jesus Christ. "Those who you counsel must come to embrace and depend on the gift and giver of grace. No one can truly change who does not know and rely on Jesus Christ our Lord." (Seeing With New Eyes by David Powlison pp. 48) Any change apart from submission to Jesus Christ is futile and counterproductive, resulting in behavior modification without a heart transformation leading to self-righteousness and self indulgence.

I. **The Pre-Existence Of Christ** - Jesus Christ existed before His birth (Micah 5:2; John 1:1-2, 14; 6:38-42; 8:52-58: 17:5; Philippians 2:5-6).

II. **The Deity Of Christ** - Christ existed as God before His birth (John 1:1; 8:58).

   A. *Proven by His names*:
   1. He is called God (John 20:28; Romans 9:5; Titus 2:13; Hebrews 1:8).
   2. He is called the Son of God (Matthew 16:16; Mark 1:1; John. 5:17-18, 10:30-36, 20:30-31).
   3. He is called Lord (Matthew 22:42-45; 1Corinthians 8:5-6).
   4. He is called King of kings and Lord of lords (Revelations 17:14, 19:16).
   5. He is called Immanuel. (Matthew 1:23).

   B. *Proven by His Characteristics*:
   1. Omnipotent (Matthew 28:18).
   2. Omniscient (John1:48, 16:30).
   3. Life (John1:4, 14:6; 1John.5:11-12).
   4. Truth (John14:6).
   5. Immutability (Hebrews 1:11-12, 13:8).
   6. Righteous (1John 2:1, 2:29, 3:7).
   7. Eternal (Hebrews 1:11-12).

C. *Proven by His Works*:

1. He created the universe (John1:3; Colossians 1:16; Hebrews 1:10; Revelations 3:14).
2. He sustains the universe (Colossians 1:17; Hebrews 1:3).
3. He gives life (John 5:21, 10:28).
4. He forgives sin (Mark 2:5-12; Luke 7:48).
5. He raises the dead (John 5:28-29, 11:43-44).
6. He will judge the human race (John 5:22-23, 27; Acts 10:42; 17:31; 2Timothy 4:1).
7. He receives worship:
    1. By angels (Hebrews 1:6).
    2. By men (Matthew 14:33; 28:17; John 9:35-38).
    3. **By all (Philippians 2:10).**

D. *Proved by His Equality*:

1. He is equal with the Father (John 5:17-18; 10:30-36; Philippians 2:6).
2. He is equal with the Holy Spirit (Matthew 28:19; 2Corinthians 13:14).

E. *The devil acknowledged His deity:*
1. Temptation… (Luke 4)

III. **The Incarnation of Christ** - Jesus Christ, the eternal second person of the Trinity took to Himself perfect and sinless humanity.

A. The *Prediction* of the Incarnation (Isaiah 7:14, 9:6).
B. The *Means* of the Incarnation: Jesus Christ became human by means of the virgin birth through Mary (Matthew 1:16-25; Luke 1:26-35; Galatians 4:4).
C. The *Result* of the Incarnation:

1. Jesus' deity was joined to perfect and sinless humanity in one person forever.
2. Jesus Christ is the God-Man (Philippians 2:5-8; Colossians 2:9).

D. The *Purpose* of the Incarnation:

1. To reveal God to man (John 1:18; 14:7-11).
2. To provide believers an example of how we are to live (1Peter 2:21-23; 1John 2:6).
3. To preach the gospel (Mark 1:38; Luke 4:18-21).
4. To save the lost (Luke 19:10; John 1:9).
5. To bear witness of the truth (John 18:37).
6. To fulfill the Davidic Covenant (Luke 1:31-33).
7. To be a merciful and faithful High Priest (Hebrews 2:17).
8. To destroy the works of the devil (Hebrews 2:14-15: 1John 3:8).
9. To provide the perfect sacrifice for sin forever (Hebrews 2:9, 16-17; 10:1-14).

10. God is spirit (John 4:24) and eternal (Genesis 21:33) and therefore, cannot die spiritually or physically. Jesus Christ became human in order to die spiritually for our sins. (Mark 15:33-34; John 19:30; Hebrews 2:9, 14, 17). He died physically in order to bring about the resurrection from the dead (Romans 6:9; 8:29; 1Corinthians 15:20-23; Philippians 3:20-21; Colossians 1:18; 1Timothy 1:10; Revelations 1:5, 18).

IV. **The Humanity of Christ:**

A. *His humanity was sinless* (Matthew 1:21; John 8:29, 46; 14:30, 18:19-23; Hebrews 4:15; 7:26).

1. The witness of the Father (Matthew 3:17; 17:5; Luke 3:22).
2. The witness of Pontius Pilate (John 18:38).
3. The witness of Pilate's wife (Matthew 27:19).
4. The witness of Judas (Matthew 27:3-4).
5. The witness of the Apostle Paul (2Corinthians 5:21).
6. The witness of the Apostle Peter (1Peter 1:19; 2:22).
7. The witness of the Apostle John (1John 3:5).
8. The witness of the thief of the cross (Luke 23:39-41).

B. *Evidence of His Humanity*:

1. He had a human body (Luke 24:39-40).
2. He ate food (Luke 24:41-43).
3. He had a human soul and spirit (Matthew 26:38; Luke 23:46).
4. He was subject to human growth and development (Luke 2:40, 52).
5. He was tired (John 4:6).
6. He slept (Mark 4:38).
7. He hungered (Mark 11:12; Luke. 4:2).
8. He wept (Luke 19:41; John 11:35).
9. He was tempted (Matthew 4:1; Mark 1:13; Luke 4:2; Hebrews 4:15).
10. He bled (John 19:34).
11. He died physically (Luke 23:46).

V. **The Work of Jesus Christ on Earth:**

A. He warned us of the detriment of our sins (John 8:34).
B. He gave us the pathway to God (John 14:6).
C. He was crucified for our sins (1Corinthians 15:3-4).
D. He was resurrected that we may have life (1Corinthians 15:20-23).

VI. **The Result of Christ's Work on Earth:**

A. *Justification* - Legally cleared us of the penalty of sin and declares us righteous. (Romans 5:1; Galatians 2:16).

B. *Reconciliation* - Restored friendship and harmony with God due to our alienation from God by sin (Romans 5:10; 2Corinthians 5:19).
C. *Propitiation* - Satisfaction of the wrath of God because of sin (1 John 2:1-2; 4:10).
D. *Sanctification* - Positional setting of believers apart from sin that they may be a part of the family of God (Hebrews 10:10).
E. *Redemption* - To be purchased, removed from bondage, and liberated (1 Corinthians 6:19-20; 1Timothy 2:6; 1Peter 1:18-19).
F. *Forgiveness* - Cancelled the debt we owed God (Colossians 2:13-14).

VII. **The Resurrection of Jesus Christ:**

A. Jesus Christ rose bodily from the dead.
B. Proved by the empty tomb (Matthew 28:1-7; Mark 16:1-6; Luke 24:1-7, 12; John 20:1-9).
C. Proved by eyewitnesses who saw, heard, touched, ate, and drank with Him after His bodily resurrection (Matthew 28:9-10, 16-17; Luke 24:13-31, 36-43; John 20:11-17, 20:19-20, 20:24-28, 21:1-14; Acts 1:1-3, 3:14-15, 10:40-41; 1Corinthians 15:4-8).
D. Benefits of Christ's Resurrection:
   1. Guarantees the believer's resurrection (Romans 6:5, 6:8-9, 26:9, 1Corinthians 15:20-23; 2Corinthians 4:14; Philippians 3:20-21; 1Thessalonians 4:13-17; 1Peter 1:3, 1 John 3:2).
   2. Christ is the believer's High Priest in heaven (Hebrews 2:17, 4:14-15, 6:19-20, 7:14-17, 7:23-25).

VIII. **The Ascension of Christ** - Forty days after His bodily resurrection, Jesus Christ ascended into heaven (Luke 24:51; Acts 1:3, 9-11; Ephesians 4:8-10; Hebrews 4:14).

IX. **The Present Ministry Of Christ In Heaven:**
A. He is seated at God the Father's right hand (Acts 2:33-35, 7:55-56; Ephesians 1:20-22; Hebrews 1:3).
B. He is the believer's merciful and faithful High Priest (Hebrews 2:17; 4:15-16; 6:19-20).
C. He intercedes for all believers (John 17:9; Romans 8:34; Hebrews 7:25).
D. He is the believer's Advocate (Romans 8:34; 1 John 2:1).
E. He is head of the church (Ephesians 1:22-23, 4:15, 5:23; Colossians 1:18; Rev. 2:3).
F. He gives spiritual gifts to the church (Ephesians 4:8-10).
G. He is preparing a place for His bride, the Church (John 14:2-3).

X. **Christ is Coming For His Church:**
A. Christ will come for His church one day. He will gather all believers, living and dead, who have believed in Him for salvation from the time of Pentecost in Acts Chapter 2 to the rapture of the Church.

B. He will gather all believers to Himself and this will end the Church Age (John 14:2-3; 1Corinthians. 15:51-53; 1Thessalonians 1:10, 4:13-17, 5:9; Revelations 22:12-13).

THE DOCTRINE OF THE HOLY SPIRIT

Key Point: The Holy Spirit is not a force or an influence, but the third Person of the Trinity (Father, Son, Holy Spirit) He is no less than but is equal in nature and character to God the Father and God the Son. He possesses the attributes of God the Father and God the Son and does the work that only God can perform (Matthew 28:19, 2Corinthians 13:14, Acts 5:3-4). The Holy Spirit leads one to know the truth, to see the reality of sin, to come to know our Lord and Savior Jesus Christ, to be able to put to death the deeds of the flesh, and to be able to walk in holiness. Biblical counseling that is led by the power of the Holy Spirit can lead individuals into these particular realities resulting in salvation and sanctification. Therefore, biblical counseling must be in line with the person and work of God the Holy Spirit in order to be a tool in the hand of God.

I. **The Person of Holy Spirit:**

    A. The Holy Spirit has a mind/intellect.(Romans 8:27)
    B. He knows and searches the things of God (1Corinthians 2:10-11, Isaiah 11:2, Ephesians 1:17)
    C. He teaches people (1Corinthians 2:12-13)
    D. The Holy Spirit has emotions. (Ephesians 4:30)
    E. He is grieved by the sinful actions of people (Ephesians 4:30).
    F. He is insulted when people reject the work of Christ (Hebrews 10:29).
    G. The Holy Spirit has a will (Romans 8:2).

II. **The Characteristics of the Holy Spirit**

    A. The Holy Spirit is Omniscient (1Corinthians 2:11-12).
    B. The Holy Spirit is Omnipresent (Psalm 139:7).
    C. The Holy Spirit is Omnipotent (Job 33:4).
    D. The Holy Spirit is called Truth (1John 5:6b).

III. **The Work of the Holy Spirit:**

    A. The Holy Spirit gives resurrection life (Romans 8:2, John 3:6).
    B. The Holy Spirit sets believers apart (2Thessalonians 2:13).
    C. The Holy Spirit comforts believers (John 14:16).
    D. The Holy Spirit gives life to creation (Job 27:3, 33:4, Psalm 104:30).
    E. The Holy Spirit gave order to creation (Isaiah 40:12, Job 26:13).
    F. The Holy Spirit is the divine author of Scripture (2Peter 1:21).

G. The Holy Spirit was the agent of the virgin birth of Jesus Christ (Luke 1:35, Matthew 1:20).
H. The Holy Spirit raised Jesus from the dead (Romans 8:11, Romans 1:4).
I. The Holy Spirit indwells believers (John 14:16-17).
J. The Holy Spirit empowers believers to live a holy life (Ephesians 5:18).
K. The Holy Spirit restrains sin from going as far as it could go (2Thessalonians 2:6-7).
L. The Holy Spirit empowers people to walk with Christ-like character (Galatians 5:16-23).
M. The Holy Spirit joins us to Christ and His people (1Corinthians 12:13).
N. The Holy Spirit seals believers in Christ (Ephesians 1:13).
O. The Holy Spirit teaches truth (John 14:26).
P. The Holy Spirit guides us into truth (John 16: 12-15).
Q. The Holy Spirit helps believers to understand truth (1Corinthians 2:10-16).
R. The Holy Spirit gives believers supernatural abilities to serve one another in the body of Christ (2Corinthians 12:1-11, Hebrews 2:4).
S. The Holy Spirit convicts believers and unbelievers of sin (John 16:7-8).
T. The Holy Spirit performs miracles (Acts 8:39).
U. The Holy Spirit testifies or witnesses (John 15:26, Romans 8:16).
V. The Holy Spirit intercedes for us to God (Romans 8:26).

IV. Conclusions for the Believer:

A. Those who walk by the Holy Spirit will experience the life and peace that surpasses explanation or understanding (Romans 8:1-11).
B. We are to put to death ungodly thoughts, words, and actions through the power of the Holy Spirit so that we will live godly lives that please and honor God (Romans 8:12-13).
C. We are to walk by the Spirit, which is submitting your thoughts, motives, desires, words, actions, relational patterns, and servce to the standards of Scripture as He empowers us to do so (Galatians 5:16-25).
D. The more we walk by the power of Holy Spirit the more He will validate our adoption into the family of God (Romans 8:14-17).

Section Five
WHAT IS TRUTH? WHAT IS THE BIBLE/SCRIPTURE?

(JOHN 18:37-38)

Key Point: Man needs truth in order to understand God, himself, creation, others, and life accordingly. Man cannot live by bread alone but by every Word that precedes out of the mouth God. Man was born with the need for direction from God before and after sin. Truth is God's mechanism to guide mankind in the direction he needs. The Word of God is the guide into knowing and understanding Truth. It is the means by which man can understand how to be set apart from the world and walk rightly with God. Genuine biblical counseling presents truth to individuals. There is no genuine biblical counsel without truth. Which means there can be no genuine biblical counseling without the Word of God. (For more on this read <u>A Theology of Christian Counseling</u> by Jay Adams.)

I. The Definition of Truth (see John 18:37-38)
- A. Objective standard by which we measure reality—that which exist.
- B. Something that is factual—that which is real, actual and accurate.
- C. Something that is right—that which is not false; that which conforms to what is correct and precise; that which is genuine.

II. The Description of Truth (see John 18:38)
- A. Truth is Absolute/Universal—that which is accurate, correct, precise, or real under all conditions without limitations to time, place, situation, color, or culture.
- B. Truth is Unified—it is not fragmented; it shows reality holistically and accurately in all aspects of life; it shows the reality of how all aspects of life connect.
- C. Truth is Abstract and Concrete—corresponds to reality that is immaterial or spiritual; corresponds to reality that is tangible or physical.

III. The Derivative of Truth (see John 1:1-2 and John 14:6)
- A. Jesus Christ is Truth.

B. Jesus Christ created all that exist visible and invisible.

C. Therefore all truth comes from Jesus Christ.

IV. The Discernment of Truth (see Romans 1:18-20, John 8:31-32, and 1John 4:1-6)
A. Truth is knowable through General Revelation—the universe; the world in which we live.

B. Truth is knowable through Special Revelation—God himself; the Word of God.

C. Truth is distinguishable from that which is a lie—untrue statements.

V. The Defense of Truth *(The Law of Non-Contradiction)*
A. Something cannot be real and not real at the same time; either it exist or it does not.

B. The opposite of what is true is false. It cannot be true and false and the same time.

C. There cannot be opposite truth claims that are both true. One has to be true and one has to be false.

VI. The Direction with Truth (see Proverbs 14:12, Galatians 6:7-8, and Proverbs 23:23)
A. Our view of life must be based on Truth or we will perish.

B. Our lifestyle must be in alignment with Truth or we will perish.

C. We must seek Truth and not reject it in all aspects of our lives.

VII. The Scripture is God's Word in written form (see 2Timothy 2:16).
A. The Scripture came from the very mouth of God (see 2Timohty 2:16).

B. God used men to write down what He said (see 2Peter 1:19-21).

C. The Scripture consist of 66 Books organized into Old and New Testament.

VIII. The Scripture is Truthful without error (see Proverbs 30:6).
A. The Scripture is pure – found to be without error (see Psalm 12:6).

B. The Scripture is the ultimate standard of truth (see John 17:17).

C. The Scripture does not affirm anything that is contrary to fact (see Psalm 19:7-11).

IX. The Scripture is a Necessity to our lives (see Psalm 119:1-16).
A. Without Scripture we would not have a full understanding of the Gospel of Jesus Christ (see 1Corinthians 15:1-11 and Romans 10:13-17).

B. Without Scripture we would not be able to understand God's agenda and how we are to live according to it (see Psalm 119:105 and 2Timothy 2:16-17).

C. Without Scripture we would not be able to maintain a godly spiritual life (see Matthew 4:4 and Psalm 119:9-11).

X. The Scripture is the Standard by which we are to govern our lives (see Psalm 1:1-3).
   A. We are to follow the commands in Scripture that are given explicitly or by implication (see 1John 2:3-6 and John 14:21).
   B. We are not to follow or obey any standard or insight that contradicts the Scripture (see Colossians 2:8, and Romans 12:2).
   C. We are to study the Scripture properly so that we may live by it accurately (see 2Timothy 2:15 and Psalm 119:33-34).

XI. Therefore we can conclude that: (John 8:31-32).
   A. You cannot know the will of God without the Word of God (see Romans 12:2).
   B. You will live a life of instability if you do not live by the Word of God (see Matthew 7:24-27).
   C. The Word of God will keep you from a sinful life or a sinful life will keep you from the Word of God (see Luke 8:11-21).

SECTION SIX

WHAT ARE HUMAN BEINGS AND HOW DID SIN IMPACT THEM?

Key Point: God created man with an immaterial and material nature. God created man with specific task and specific ways to relate with God, each other and creation (A Theology of Christian Counseling pp. 100). Without understanding God's design and purpose for mankind, one may think they are able to live their own way without any regard for God. This leads to confusion, disorder and utter destruction of man and society. When man interprets life apart from God it will result in a wrong view of the nature of man leading to an unbiblical view and practice of life (see Proverbs 14:12, Proverbs 28:26, Jeremiah 17:5-6, 9-10, and Romans 1:21-23). A biblical view of man helps one to develop a biblical view and practice of life (see Genesis 1:26-27, 2:7, Ecclesiastes 7:29, Mark 7:14-23, 1Corinthains 1:21-31, and Colossians 3:1-17). Knowing sin's impact on mankind can take the mystery out of the pain and suffering we encounter in life. It can help us understand why man lives the way he does and what changes he needs to function as he was intended. Genuine biblical counseling embraces the biblical view of man and leads individuals into understanding and living according to that view. Counseling that articulates a view of man as autonomous or self-sufficient is contradictory to God's design and will lead men to more bondage. If one is going to practice genuine biblical counseling, he/she must learn the biblical view of human beings.

I. Human Beings were created by God (see Genesis 1:26).
   A. Human beings are a creation of God designed in God's image (see Genesis 1:26-27).
   B. Human beings have been created male and female (see Genesis 1:26-27).
   C. Human beings were created dependent on God in all things (see Acts 17:24-28).
   D. Human beings were created with the capacity to relate with God and others (see 1John 4:20-21).
   E. Human being were originally created good (see Genesis 1:31).
   F. Human beings have been created as eternal beings that will live forever either in Fellowship with God, or in eternal damnation (see Luke 16:19-31, John 3:36, and Revelation 20:11-15).

II. Human Beings were created with immaterial and material distinctives (see Genesis 2:7).
   A. Human beings have been designed with a mind, which involves our thoughts, beliefs, understanding, memory, judgment, imaginations, discernment and conscience (see Proverbs 23:7, Romans 12:2-3, Romans 2:15-16, Mark 2:6, and 2Corinthians 10:5).
   B. Human beings have been designed with affections, which involves our longings, desires, and feelings (see Psalm 20:4, Ecclesiastes 7:9, 11:9, Psalm 73:7, James 3:14, Hebrews 12:3, and Joshua 14:8).
   C. Human beings have been designed with a will, which involves our ability to choose and determine action (see Deuteronomy 30:19, Joshua 24:15, Psalm 25:12, and Ecclesiastes 2:4-8).
   D. Our mind, affections, and will, are the sum total of what we call the immaterial part of man (non-physical); the bible generally uses the words soul, spirit, and heart when speaking of the immaterial aspect of man (see 1Corinthains 2:11, Roman 8:16, and Proverbs 4:23). (Sometimes the word soul is used to describe the whole person both material and immaterial (see Acts 2:41.)
   E. Human beings have been designed with a physical body, which is the home of the immaterial part of us. (see 2Corinthains 5:1-10, Philippians 1:19-23, 1Corinthains 9:27, and 1Corinthians 15:35-58).
   F. The physical body and immaterial part of human beings are an inseparable union while man is alive on earth (see Genesis 2:7, 1Corinthians 15:35-38, and Philippians 1:19-23).

III. Human Beings were created for the Purpose of (see Isaiah 43:7):
   A. Reflecting God's character in all things (see 1Corinthains 10:31 and Matthew 5:14-16).
   B. Worshipping God in spirit and in truth (see John 4:23-24 and Deuteronomy 6:13-15).
   C. Knowing God intimately through fellowship with Him and with others (see John 17:3, Jeremiah 9:23-24, and 1John 4:19-21).
   D. Delighting in the excellence of God's Character (Psalm 37: 4 and Psalm 84:1-10).
   E. Being useful to God according to our unique design, roles, and responsibilities given by God to us (see 2Timothy 2:20-21 and Ephesians 2:10).
   F. Managing the creation (see Genesis 1:26-28 and Genesis 2:15-17).

IV. Therefore we can conclude that (see John 15:1-6):
   A. Mankind was designed to live for God and not independent of Him.
   B. Mankind's understanding of the purpose for life can only come from God.

C. Mankind's true purpose for relationships can only come from God.

D. Mankind's true purpose for life will never come from pleasure, prosperity, independence or materialism.

E. Mankind's value cannot not be determined by other people but by God.

F. Mankind's destiny can only be determined by God not man.

V. The First Man Adam and First Woman Eve fell into sin (disobedience to God) (Genesis 3:1-24)

A. Adam and Eve chose to doubt the command given them by God.

B. Adam and Eve chose to distrust the command given them by God.

C. Adam and Eve chose to disengage from the command given them by God.

D. Adam and Eve chose to disobey the command given them by God.

E. Adam and Eve chose to deny their sinful behavior to God.

F. Adam and Eve chose to defend their sinful behavior to God.

VI. The Sin of Adam and Eve ruined life for all mankind

A. As a result of Adam's sin all of mankind was imputed with sin – placed in the position of sinner before God; considered by position in life a sinner (Romans 5:12-21, 3:10).

B. As a result of Adam's sin all of mankind is born with inherited sin – we are born with a heart that is against God; we are born with a sin-infested nature; we are naughty by nature; we are born with a sin condition (Psalm 51:5, Jeremiah 17:9, Genesis 6:5, Matthew 15:15-20, Romans 8:7, Romans 7:7-24).

C. As a result of Adam's sin all of mankind walks in individual sin before God and others (Romans 3:10-18, 23, Ecclesiastes 7:20, Romans 8:5-8).

D. As a result of Adam's sin mankind experiences spiritual death - separation from the influence of God's power, presence, and promises; separation from the indwelling of God in them, separation from fellowship and communication with God; under the control of the devil and his system of living (Ephesians 2:1-5).

E. As a result of Adam's sin mankind experiences physical death – the spirit of man is separated from the physical body when physical life ceases (James 2:26).

F. As a result of Adam's sin mankind experiences eternal death – separation from God forever after physical death into eternal punishment and damnation (Revelation 20:4-15, John 3:16-18).

G. As a result of Adam's sin all of mankind tends to worship self and creation above God (Romans 1:18-32, 2Timothy 3:1-5, Luke 12:13-21).

H. As a result of Adams sin all of mankind is an enemy of God until they come to Jesus Christ for forgiveness of sin and salvation (Romans 5:10).

I. As a result of Adam's sin mankind in general has become helpless, useless, and a slave to sin apart from salvation in Jesus Christ (Romans 3:10-18, Romans 8:5-8, Romans 7:7-24).

J. As a result of Adam's sin, mankind has sought to set themselves up as autonomous beings; Trying to redefine good and evil according to their own standard and live apart from God (see Psalm 14:1-3).

K. As a result of Adam's sin mankind has lost the ability to know themselves accurately (see Jeremiah 17:9).

L. As a result of Adam's sin mankind has lost the ability to judge the universe accurately making it a god to worship instead of a responsibility to manage (see Romans 1:18-25).

M. As a result of Adam's sin mankind's ability to reason is marred there by weakening their ability to discern good and evil (see Proverbs 14:12).

N. As a result of Adam's sin mankind seeks to use people and love things instead of loving people and using things (see Romans 1:18-25).

O. As a result of Adam's sin, imagination has become vain and separate from reality—illusion (see Psalm 73:7).

VII. As a result of the Sin Choice of Adam and Eve mankind has a distorted view of himself (See Proverbs 16:25, and Ecclesiastes 7:29.)

A. Because of sin, man has reasoned himself to believe that he is basically good and that society is bad. Therefore, bad behavior is a result of a bad society not a sinful nature in man.

B. This leads man to believe that society needs to be reconstructed not that man needs to be redeemed and sanctified (He is basically good).

C. This leads man to believe that people can be shaped and manipulated like objects to fit a society as needed.

D. This leads man to believe that social problems are not moral problems but technical problems to be addressed by scientific solutions.

E. As a result of this deceived thinking man is lead to the idea that, social planners and controllers are the key to remaking human nature and society.

F. As a result of this deceived thinking, the soul, conscience, moral reasoning and moral responsibility are not issues to be concerned with.

G. Therefore their conclusion is that the direction of mankind and the culture rest in the hands of social scientist and the government not God.

(Concepts A-G adapted from How Now Shall We Live? By Charles Colson)

Section Seven
What Is the Gospel?

Key Point: Christians are called to be Ambassadors for Jesus Christ to a world of people who do not follow Jesus Christ. We have been given the ministry of reconciliation with intent of making Disciples of Jesus Christ (2 Corinthians 5:18-21). As ambassadors, Christians seek to explain to unbelievers the reality that all have sinned and need to be saved from the coming judgment of Jesus Christ on unbelievers (non-followers of Jesus Christ) as a result of their sin. As ambassadors, Christians seek to persuade unbelievers to repent of sin and be reconciled to God through faith in the person and work of Jesus Christ resulting in being saved from the penalty, power and soon presence of sin unto a genuine relationship with God where they are made righteous as result Christ taking their penalty and punishment for sin resulting in becoming a Disciple of Jesus Christ. Genuine biblical counseling seeks to share the Gospel with unbelievers knowing that true deliverance and change cannot happen without reconciliation to God. Counseling that does not embrace the Gospel of Jesus Christ is not helpful but detrimental to mankind. It leaves mankind with the idea that deliverance and change can happen apart from God through personal efforts. Everyone who practices biblical counseling must know and develop in the presentation of the Gospel of Jesus Christ.

I. Disciples of Jesus Christ are made by God as He wills, as we present the Gospel (Good News) of Jesus Christ to people who are not followers of Jesus Christ (1 Corinthians 3:5-9).Therefore, we must know and understand the Gospel of Jesus Christ (1 Corinthians 15:1-4):

   A. Jesus Christ who is God and the Son of God took on the form of a man (John 1:14-18, Philippians 2:5-11).

   B. Jesus Christ took on the form of a man to pay the penalty for sins of the human race (Hebrews 10:1-18).

   C. Through Christ's physical death on the Cross, literal burial and resurrection from physical death, Jesus paid the penalty for the sins of mankind (Acts 2:22-36).

D. Christ's physical death on the Cross, literal burial, and resurrection from physical death results in deliverance from the penalty of sin and power of sin for those who put their faith(trust or confidence) in the person and work of Jesus Christ (Romans 5:1- 6:15).

E. Christ's physical death on the Cross, literal burial and resurrection from physical death results in deliverance from the presence of sin for those who put their faith(trust or confidence) in the person and work of Jesus Christ (Revelation 21:1-27).

F. Christ's physical death on the Cross, literal burial and resurrection from physical death results in receiving a resurrected heavenly body like Jesus and being with Him forever for those who put their faith (trust or confidence) in the person and work of Jesus Christ (Philippians 3:17-21).

G. Christ's physical death on the Cross, literal burial, and resurrection from physical death results in receiving a salvation unto a right relationship with God the Father that last eternally for those who put their faith (trust or confidence) in the person and work of Jesus Christ. This salvation is to motivate one to know God intimately, to become like Him, and to be useful to Him practically. (Romans 5:1-2, John 17:3, Philippians 3:7-11, Ephesians 4:17-24, 2:1-10, John 15:1-5).

II. **A proper response to the Gospel of Jesus Christ results in one becoming a Disciple of Jesus Christ. Here is an example of proper response to the Gospel of Jesus Christ (1Corinthains 15:1-4):**

A. We are to listen to the validity of the Gospel message (Romans 10:1-17).

B. We are to affirm the message by accepting the reality of our sinfulness and our need to be forgiven of our sin; We should then to turn from sin to put our faith (trust or confidence) in the person and work of Jesus Christ to deliver us from our sin unto a right relationship with God the Father (2Corinthians 7:10-11).

C. We are to be steadfast in the conviction that we are saved eternally from the penalty of sin, the power of sin and soon the presence of sin as a result of putting our faith (trust or confidence) in the person and work of Jesus Christ (Romans 5:1- 6:1-15).

D. We are to be steadfast in the hope of the return of Jesus Christ knowing that when He returns we will receive a heavenly body like Christ's since we have put our faith (trust or confidence) in the person and work of Jesus Christ (Philippians 3:17-21, Romans 8:18-25).

E. We are to be steadfast in the conviction that we are saved unto a right relationship with God the Father that will last eternally as a result of putting our faith (trust or confidence) in the person and work of Jesus Christ (John 3:16, 17:3, Romans 5:1- 8:39).

F. As a result of trusting or putting our confidence in the Gospel message resulting in an eternally secure salvation, there should be a desire to pursue and know God intimately resulting in seeking to learn how to walk with Jesus Christ. This should result in one learning to live by faith working itself out in obedience to God and love for others. If this is not happening it means that we didn't have a genuine/sincere faith or we have forgotten that we have been purified from our sins to live for Jesus Christ (2Corinthains 5: 15, Galatians 2:20, Philippians 3:1-16, Romans 5:1-8:39, Galatians 5:1-25, 2Peter 1:1-11).

III. If a person rejects the Gospel of Jesus Christ he will suffer the consequences of sin forever (John 8:12-24)

A. If mankind rejects the Gospel of Jesus Christ he will be an enemy to God forever (Romans 5:10).

B. If mankind rejects Gospel of Jesus Christ he will be a slave to the condition of inherited sin while alive (Matthew 15:15-20, Romans 7:5).

C. If mankind rejects the Gospel Jesus Christ he will be given over to self-destruction (Romans 1:18-32).

D. If mankind rejects the Gospel of Jesus Christ he will never find his intended purpose for existence (Matthew 16:24-28).

E. If mankind rejects the Gospel of Jesus Christ he has nothing else or no one else who can save him (Act 4:5-12).

F. If mankind rejects the Gospel of Jesus Christ he will experience eternal death – separation from God forever after physical death into eternal punishment and damnation (Revelation 20:4-15, John 3:16-18).

SALVATION

Key Point: Salvation- Deliverance from the penalty, power and soon the presence of sin through the death burial and resurrection of Jesus Christ unto a right relationship with God the Father (John1:12, Ephesians1:4-7, 2:8-10, 1Corinthians 15:1-3; 1 Peter 1:18-19).Through salvation in Jesus Christ mankind will: gain spiritual life – connection to the influence of God's power, presence, and promises; indwelling presence of God; fellowship and communication with God (Ephesians 2:1-22, Ephesians 1:13-14), gain eternal life – connection in relationship and fellowship with God forever (John 17:3), be forgiven of his sin against God (1John 2:1-2), be placed into the family of God (Ephesians 2:11-19), made useful and productive for God's agenda (Ephesians 2:8-10, Romans 7:4), given the Holy Spirit to indwell him so that he may have power to live a life that is pleasing to God (Romans 7:24-8:17, Romans 1:13-14), and become a pleaser of God (Galatians 1:10, Philippians 3:1-21). Genuine biblical counseling seeks to lead one into embracing salvation. Counsel that does not seek to deal with sin in order to lead one into salvation and sanctification is not biblical counseling. Counsel that does not move one in the direction of eternal life will keep one captive to eternal death.

I. The Components of Salvation:

  A. Election- God in His sovereignty grants salvation to totally depraved sinners as He decided before the foundation of the world. It was not based on the person, it was decided by God. Those whom He granted salvation will repent and trust Christ as Savior (Romans 9:1-33, John 6:43, 65, Ephesians 1:4-11, John 1:12-13, 3:16-18).

  B. Regeneration- The Holy Spirit makes us alive in Christ. We receive a new power, position, and passion to obey God, relate to God and bear fruit for Him (John 3:3-8, Titus 3:1-10, Ephesians 2:1-10, 2 Corinthians 5:14-17, Colossians 2:11-14, Romans 7:4).

  C. Justification- It is an act of God whereby He declares man judicially right before Him. He set us free from the penalty of sin through the sacrifice of Jesus Christ. Through faith in Jesus Christ, man is made at peace with God—No longer His enemy (Romans 5:1, Romans 3:20-31, Colossians 2:13-14).

  D. Adoption- God made us a part of his family; we have become the Children of God (Romans 8:14-17, John 1:12, Ephesians 2:11-22, Galatians 3:23-26, 4:1-7, 1John 3:1-2, Hebrews 2:10-18).

  E. Sanctification– It is the process by which God works within a Christian's heart so that he or she will become like Jesus Christ in all aspects of his or her life. A Christian responds to that power from within his or her heart by walking more in the ways of God and less in ways of sin in all aspects of life resulting in becoming a mature person in Christ in every area of his or her life. God makes the Christian a Saint in position and empowers the Christian to progressively become a Saint in practice resulting in the comprehensive and complete transformation of the Christian into the image of Jesus Christ. (Hebrews 10:10,14, 1Corinthians 6:11, 1 Corinthians 1:2, 1 Peter 1:1-2, Philippians 2:12-13, Hebrews 12:1-14,13:20-21, 1Thessalonians 5:23, Romans 8:13, Romans 6:1-21, 1 John 3:1-3, Ephesians 4:17-32).

F. *Perseverance*– Those who truly belong to Christ are kept by God's power and will continue in the faith unto Heaven (John 6:38-40, Philippians 1:6, 1Peter 1:1-6, Matthew 10:22, Colossians 1:22-23, Hebrews 3:14).

G. *Security*– Man cannot lose his salvation; it is given by God and secured by God (John 3:16-18,36, 5:24, 6:37-40,10:27-29, 1John 5:13, Philippians 1:6, 1Peter 1:1-5, Romans 5:9-10, 8:1-39, Ephesians 1:13-14).

II. Evidence that neither validates nor invalidates that one is saved:

A.	Visible Morality	Romans 10:1-4
B.	Intellectual Knowledge	James 2:18-26
C.	Religious Involvement	Matthew 7:21-24
D.	Active Ministry	Matthew 7:21-24
E.	Conviction of Sin	2Corinthians 7:9-10
F.	Assurance	John 8:39-59
G.	Time of Decision	Luke 8:13, 14

III. Evidence that validates ones salvation is authentic:

A. Repentance from Sin	Psalm 32:5, Proverbs 28:13, Romans 6:1-22 Romans 8:12-13, 2Corinthians 7:9-11, 1John 1:8-10, Psalm 51, Galatians 5:24
B. Separation From the sinful living	Galatians 2:20, 5:24, 1John 4:1-6, Titus 2:11-14, Romans 12:1-2, 2Corinthians 6:14-7:1, 1John 2:15-17, James 3:13-4:10
C. Obedient Living	John 14:15,21, 1John 4:15-21, 1John 2:3-6, 1John 3:1-10, Galatians 5:16-23, John 15:1-17
D. Love for Others	1John 3:13-24, 1John 4:7-21, John 13:35

E. Desire to know God   Psalm 42:1-2, Psalm 73:25, Philipians 3:7-10

F. Anticipation of His Return   1John 3:1-3, Philippians 3:17-21, 1Peter 1:1-6

G. Being faithful over your   Romans 12:3-8, 1Peter 4:10-11
   Spiritual Gifts

H. Committed to evangelism   Matthew 28:18-20, 2Corinthians 5:11-21
   and discipleship

IV. So how does one receive this salvation from God?

A. You must believe that there is only One God who created heaven and earth and He exists eternally in three persons (God the Father, Son, Holy Spirit) (Deuteronomy 6:4, Genesis 1:1, John 1:1-12, Matthew 28:19).

B. You must believe that you are a sinner that deserves God's Judgment (Romans 5:12-14, Psalm 51:5, Romans 3:23, Romans 6:23).

C. You must put your trust/confidence in the fact that Jesus Christ, who is fully God and fully man came out of heaven to earth and was crucified, buried and arose on the third day to pay the penalty for your sin. (Romans 4:25, Romans 5:8, 1 Corinthians 15:1-5, Philippians 2:1-11).

D. You must have a change of mind, purpose, and direction from sin (repent) to trust in Jesus Christ (God the Son) to save you from the penalty, power, and presence of sin and to sanctify you unto a right relationship with God the Father (John 1:12, John 3:1-21, 2Corinthians 7:10-11, Titus 2:11-14, Acts 20:17-21, Acts 17:30-34, Romans 2:1-4).

Summary

Mankind needs God in order to escape the consequences of sin. Mankind needs God in order to live a life in the presence of God that was designed for him by God before the fall of Adam into sin (resulting in all of mankind falling into sin). God did not create mankind to live for himself. Nor did God create mankind to live independent of Him. Mankind's purpose for existence can only be discovered through a right relationship with God. Mankind's forgiveness of sin can only be received through salvation in Jesus Christ. God created the world and all that exist in it. Therefore, any attempt to live independent of the Creator in thoughts, words, actions, relationship patterns, or lifestyle will result in total devastation for those who reject God's order, design, and will for life (Proverbs 5:21-23). Just remember that all have sinned (Romans 3:23), the penalty for sin is death (Romans 6:23), and that Jesus Christ, who is God and who was sent by God the Father, came down out of heaven and took on the form of man to pay the penalty for our sins (Colossians 2:8-15).

If you acknowledge the truth about your sin condition before God, the deserved punishment you should receive for your sin, repent of your sin, and put your faith (confidence) in this truth about who Jesus Christ is, where He came from, and what he has done for you, you shall be saved from the penalty, power, and presence of sin unto a right standing/relationship with God the Father. Through salvation in Christ you will have power to know God and live in His presence according to His will (Romans 3:23,4:25, 5:1-21, 6:1-23,8:1-39,10:9-10, 1Corinthians 15: 1-58, Philippians 2:5-11, John 3:16-18 14:1-14,8:12-59, 1John 4:1-15, Proverbs 28:13-14, 2Corinthians 5:11-21, 7:10, Titus 2:11-15,3:1-8).

Contrast between the Saved and the Unsaved

Unsaved (In Adam)	Saved (In Christ)
•Spiritual Death (Ephesians 2:1-2)	•Spiritual Life (Ephesians 2:4-5)
•Imputed Sin (Romans 5:12-14, 18)	•Imputed Righteousness (Romans 5:15-19; 2 Corinthians 5:21)
•Inherited Sin and Individual Sins (Romans 3:10, 23, Psalm 51:5)	•Indwelling Spirit (Ephesians 1:13-14)
•Sinners (Romans 5:8, 19)	•Saints (Ephesians 1:1; Philippians 1:1)
•Unforgiven (John 8:24)	•Forgiven (Ephesians 1:7)
•Enemies of God (Romans 5:10)	•Reconciled to God (Romans 5:10-11)
•Guilty Lawbreakers (Romans 3:23)	•Justified (Romans 3:24)
•Physical Death (1 Corinthians 15:22a)	•Physical Resurrection (1 Corinthians 15:22b)
•Eternal Death (Revelation 20:4-15)	•Eternal Life (John 3:16)

Chart by Gaylon Clark

(People who are not saved are considered to be in Adam and are, therefore, still subject to the negative effects of Adam's sin. Their identity is drawn from their relationship to Adam, the head of the family. People who are saved are considered to be in Christ and therefore, enjoy the benefits of salvation provided by Christ through His Death. Their identity is drawn from their relationship to Christ who is their family head.)

Section Eight

The Definition and Components of Mortification and Sanctification

Key Point: God saved us from the consequences of sin to sanctify us. Sanctification is the end result of being changed into the perfect likeness of Jesus Christ. We were transitioned from sinner to be transformed into a Saint. We were delivered to be developed. Even though sanctification is the work of God, He involves man in the process. God has set Christians apart to Himself and empowered Christians to participate with Him in the process of making them like Him. God works in Christians and on Christians. As a result he expects Christians to respond to that work through a life of disciplined obedience. Christians are to be devoted to putting off sin in their lives according to the power of Holy Spirit who works within them (Romans 8:1-14), and are to be devoted to walking in holiness according to the power of the Holy Spirit that works within them. Christians are to spend their lives becoming in practice what they are in position through the power of God within them. (1John 3:1-3, Romans 8:1-14). In genuine biblical counseling this process is facilitated. In order for one to practice effective biblical counseling he must know and learn the premise and practice of mortification and sanctification as well as the essential elements involved.

I. What Mortification is Not

A. Mortification is not trying to restrain the physical body which is the instrument of sin not the source of sin (Romans 6:12-13).[1]
B. Mortification is not completely destroying sin.[2]
C. Mortification is not diverting to something else and assuming that sin problem has gone away.[3]
D. Mortification is not changing from one sin to some lesser sin.[4]

---

[1] Sinclair B. Ferguson, *The Christian Life: A Doctrinal Introduction* (London: Hodder and Stoughton, 1981),158

[2] Ibid., 158

[3] Ibid, *162*

E. Mortification is not having a quiet peaceful temperament due to self righteousness (Romans 2:14-15).[5]

II. The Definition of Mortification

A. Mortification is the refusal to allow the eye to wander after anything or anyone that will draw one from Jesus Christ.[6]
B. Mortification is the refusal to allow the mind to contemplate anything or anyone that will draw one from Jesus Christ.[7]
C. Mortification is the refusal to allow the affections to run after anything or anyone that will draw one from Jesus Christ.[8]
D. Mortification is the deliberate rejection of any sinful thought, suggestion, desire, aspiration, deed, circumstance or provocation that will draw one away from Jesus Christ at the moment one becomes aware of it.[9]
E. Mortification is the consistent endeavor to do all in one's power to weaken the grip of sin in one's life.[10]

III. The Practice of Mortification

A. Identify sin in the thought, attitude, motivation, conversation, behavior, lifestyle and relational patterns.
B. Bring sin into the light of God's presence and agree with God it is sin (confession) (1John1:9).[11]
C. Recall the shame of the past sin by remembering the detriment it caused you then (Romans 6:20-21).[12]
D. Remember you are united with Jesus Christ with a new position, power, purity, and passion to live in your new life with Christ (2Corinthians 5:15-17, Romans 6:1-21).[13]

---

[4] Ibid, *162*

[5] Ibid, *162*

[6] Ibid, *162*

[7] Ibid, *162*

[8] Ibid, *162*

[9] Ibid, *163*

[10] Ibid, *163*

[11] Ibid, *166-167*

[12] Ibid, *166-167*

[13] Ibid, *166-167*

E. Resist and turn away from the sin accordingly (Proverbs 28:13).

IV. The Means and Goal of Mortification

A. Mortification is only possible through the power of the Holy Spirit (Romans 8:13)
B. The Holy Spirit gives us the power to resist sin (Galatians 5:16).
C. Mortification is the means by which we can move into sanctification (Romans 6:12-22).
D. Mortification is the means by which we can move into experiencing eternal life (Galatians 5:24, Romans 8:13, Galatians 6:7-8)
E. Mortification is the means by which we begin to see the hope of what we will be in Jesus Christ (1John 3:1-3)

V. The Definition of Sanctification

A. Sanctification is the same Greek word as holiness, "*hagios*," meaning a separation.[14]
B. Sanctification consists in the removal of the "penal consequences of sin from the moral nature and the progressive implanting and growth of a new principle of life."[15]
C. It is not just "deliverance from sin but development of a life that reflects the very character of God."[16]
D. It is the "carrying on to perfection the work begun in regeneration, which extends to the whole man."[17]
E. The separation from evil unto God, in position, condition, and life unto the very likeness of Jesus Christ.

VI. Sanctification is Divided into Three Categories

A. Sanctification is a "once-for-all" positional separation unto Christ at our salvation.[18]
B. Sanctification is a "practical progressive holiness" in a believer's life while awaiting the return of Christ.
C. Sanctification is "the end result of being changed into the perfect likeness of Jesus Christ set apart in character and completely separated from the presence of evil."[19]

---

[14]"What is Sanctification?" [on-line]; accessed 5 November 2009; available from http://gotquestions.org/sanctification.html; Internet.

[15]Augustus Hopkins Strong, *Systematic Theology: A Compendium and Commonplace-Book Designed for the Use of Theological Students* (Rochester, NY: Press of E. R. Andrews, 1886), 869

[16]A. A. Hodge, "Providence," in *Outlines of Theology*, ed. Edward N. Gross, (Carlisle, PA: The Banner of Truth Trust, 1983), 343

[17]M. G. Easton, *Easton's Bible Dictionary* (Logos Research System; reprint, Oak Harbour, WA: Public Domain, 1996, c1897) "n. p."

[18]Ibid.

[19]Ibid.

VII. The Work of Sanctification

A. Sanctification is a work of God.

B. God the Father carries out the work of sanctification through the Holy Spirit who indwells Christians.[20]

C. Even though sanctification is a work of God, He invites Christians to be involved in the process (Phil 2:12-13).

D. Christians are to be devoted to putting off sinful patterns of living in thoughts, desires, words, actions and walking in holiness through the power of God (1 John 3:1-3, Eph 4:17- 24).

E. As God works, Christians are to respond by working out in practice what He is doing in them, for them and through them (Phil 2:12-13).

F. They are working from their new position in Christ in contradiction to their old position under Adam in sin; God has set Christians apart to Himself and empowered Christians to participate with God in the process of making Christians like Him in character (Rom 5:1-6:22).

VIII. The Word of God on Sanctification

A. In 1 Corinthians 6:11, the Apostle Paul emphasized the position of sanctification. He used words such as washed, sanctified, and justified. These words were used to emphasize different sides of the reality of being set apart for God.[21]

B. In 1 John 3:1-3, John communicated to the Christians that they were children of God. These Christians were called to accept the fact that their name set them apart from the godless system of the world.

C. In 1 Timothy 4:7-10, Paul challenged Timothy to stay away from false teaching and pursue Godliness anticipating the fullness of salvation to come.

D. In Philippians 2:12-13, Paul encouraged the Philippians to be God-pleasers instead of man- pleasers.[22] The saints could obey without the presence of Paul because it was God at work within them. God was energizing the Saints with their desire and ability to obey.[23]

E. In Ephesians 4:17-24, Paul challenged those Christians to live their lives according to their new position in Jesus Christ. They were challenged to no longer live the way they lived before they were placed in Jesus Christ. What one was in position was to be reflected in how one lived in practice.

---

[20] Strong, *Systematic* Theology, 871.

[21] Charles Hodge, *Commentary on 1 & 2 Corinthians.* (Edinburgh: Banner of Truth Trust, 1974), 63.

[22] J. B. Lightfoot, The Epistles of St. Paul III: The First Roman Captivity, *Saint Paul's Epistle to the Philippians*, A Revised Text with Introduction, Notes and Dissertations, (London: Macmillan, 1896).

[23] Wuest, Kenneth S.: *Wuest's Word Studies from the Greek New Testament : For the English Reader*. Grand Rapids : Eerdmans, 1997, c1984, S. 1 Ti 4:7-9 "n. p."

F. In Colossians 3:1-17 Paul went into detail in explaining the purpose and practice of progressive sanctification. He reasoned with the church to put off particular sinful patterns as a result of their position in Christ, their prize in Christ, and the Person of Christ. In addition, Paul reasoned with the church to put off particular sinful patterns and walk in their new character in Christ, knowing they were being transformed into the image of Jesus Christ as result. He also reasoned with the church to put on attitudes and actions that reflect the character of Christ and as a result being chosen, made holy, and being the object of God's affections.

Section Nine

The Essence of Spiritual Development and Maturity

Key Point: When you evaluate Scripture, you will find that when we are called to change it comes back to thoughts, attitudes, desires, intention, conversation, lifestyle, serving and relational patterns. It cannot be ignored if real change is going to take place. No one else can be responsible to obedience or for disobedience of an individual in these areas of life but the person themselves. People may have had influence in these areas but man controls his own choices in these areas (Galatians 6:7-8). Therefore no one can blame anyone for the choices they have made in these areas. Man has to be delivered from his sin condition by God in order to obey God in these key areas of life. The steps of change are the normal progression of Christians as they develop through the sanctification process into the likeness of Jesus Christ as empowered by God. The spiritual growth stages are the categories used to define periods of time and to determine what has to be done through the Word of God to move someone to or through those particular periods of time. This is not a smooth process. Genuine biblical counseling involves itself in facilitating this process as it hones in on the essential areas of life that have to be addressed if change into the image of Jesus Christ is going to take place.

Definition of Spiritual Maturity: To be fully developed in character and faith in Jesus Christ (Colossians 1:28-29, Ephesians 4:11-15).

I. **The Prize of Spiritual Maturity:**
   A. To know God intimately to the fullest measure (John 17:3, Ephesians 3:14-20).
   B. To be like Jesus Christ in every aspect of your life to the fullest measure (Ephesians 4:11-15).
   C. To be useful and productive in your service to God to the fullest measure (Romans 7:4, John 15:5).
   D. To develop a life that reflects love for God and Love for others to the fullest measure (John 14:21. 1John 2:3-11, 4:7-21).

II. **The Particulars of Spiritual Development:**
   A. We are to develop godly thinking patterns and motives (Romans 12:2).
   B. We are to develop godly desires (Matthew 6:19-22, Colossians 3:1-5).
   C. We are to develop godly communication patterns (Ephesians 4:29).
   D. We are to develop godly behavioral patterns (Ephesians 4:17-32).
   E. We are to develop godly relational patterns (Colossians 3:12-14).
   F. We are to develop godly serving patterns (John 13:1-17).

III. **The Process of Spiritual Development:**
   A. God is saving **_souls_** from the power, penalty, and soon the presence of sin (Ephesians 2:1-10, Colossians 1:12-14).

   B. God is maturing **_Saints_** into the image of Jesus Christ (2Corinthains 3:18, Romans 8:29-30).

   C. God is using the **_Church_** through evangelism to save souls (2Corinthians 5:18-20, Colossians 1:3-6).

   D. God is using the **_Church_** through discipleship to mature saints into the image of Christ (Matthew 28:18-20, Ephesians 4:11-15).

   E. God is working inside of you (Philippians 2:12-13).
      1. He is challenging your thoughts (Philippians 3:13-15).
      2. He is convicting you of sin (Philippians 3:13-15).
      3. He is revealing the truth about life to you (2 Corinthians 2:9-16, John 16:8-13).
      4. He is giving you power to live, to serve, and to enjoy life (2 Peter 1:1-10).
      5. He is guiding you into His will (John 16:13).
      6. He is changing you into the image of Jesus Christ (2 Corinthians 3:18, Philippians 3:20-21).
   F. As God is working within your heart, you are to respond accordingly (Philippians 2:12-13)

   G. There are **_six steps_** that demonstrate that you are responding accordingly as God is working inside of you. These steps result in spiritual maturity taking place in your life.

   1. **_Realization_** - One comes to see truth and understand how it applies to their life (2Timothy 2:24-26).

   2. **_Remorse_** - One comes to feel godly sorrow in relation to their sin and desire to make things right with God and others accordingly.(2 Corinthians 7:10).

   3. **_Renounce_** - One comes to confess their sin to God and to others when appropriate (Psalm 32:1-11, James 5:16).

4. ***Repentance*** - One comes to turn away from their sin towards God and towards others accordingly (Proverbs 28:13, 2Corinthians 7:10-11).

5. ***Renewal*** - One comes to meditate on the truth so that he/she may learn the new direction by which he/she is to obey God and love others accordingly (Ephesians 4:17-23).

6. ***Replacement*** - One comes to obey God and love others in the area where he/she has disobeyed God and been unloving towards others (Ephesians 4:17-23).

H. Each ***step of change*** is worked out through ***stages of spiritual growth*** (2 Timothy 3:16).

 1. **Teaching Stage**: The Holy Spirit guides, convicts and enlightens your mind through the Word of God, the Body of Christ, circumstances, and prayer (John 16:8-13, 1Corinthians 2:9-12, Hebrews 4:12, 1John 4:4-6, 1Peter 4:12-13, (Romans 8:26-27) (Realization occurs as a result.).

 2. **Conviction Stage**: God begins to focus your attention in particular areas of life convincing you that change is necessary. (Philippians 3:14-15, 2Corinthians 7:10-11) (Realization and Remorse occurs as a result.).

 3. **Correction Stage**: You make a decision to abandon a sin issue and begin a new thought, word, or action trusting God's power to make things function accordingly (2Corinthians 7:10-11, Proverbs 28:13-14) (Renounce and Repentance occurs as a result.).

 4. **Training Stage**: As you are responding to God's conviction you are seeking to put to practice what God has commanded in His Word
    a. By the power of God you are walking in harmony with God in areas where you were once disobedient.
    b. You are experiencing victory: a deeper fellowship with God and with others (2Peter 1:1-11, Proverbs 12:13, 24:16, John 8:31-32, Luke 8:4-18, Ephesians 4:11-13, 1John 3:1-3). (Renewal and Replacement occurs as a result.).

I. The Community of Faith in Jesus Christ is to help each member through each step and stage by:

1. helping members look closely at and work hard on having a ***thought life, motives, and desires*** that are pleasing to God as God's Word commands (Romans 12:2-3, 2Corinthian 10:3-5, Matthew 6:19-22, Colossians 3:1-5).

2. helping members look closely at work hard on ***communicating*** in ways that are honest and edifying to others as God's Word commands (Ephesians 4:29).

3. helping members look closely at and work hard on walking in **_behavior_** that is consistent with Christ's Character as God's Word commands (Ephesians 4:17-32, 5:1-17, Galatians 5:16-26).

4. helping members look closely at and work hard on **_relating_** to others in ways that demonstrate the love of Christ as God's Word commands (Romans 12: 9-21, 13:8-12).

5. helping members look closely at and work hard on **_serving_** others in ways that will bear their burdens and meet their needs as God's Word commands (Ephesians 4:11-16, 1Peter 4:10-11).

6. leading individuals into:

    - **_Membership_** – individuals would be lead to join a local church that they may experience love and enjoy the blessings of God-honoring relationships.

    - **_Maturity_** – individuals would be lead to get involved in discipleship courses in a local Church that would lead them into loving God, loving others on a consistent basis and living a life that reflects the character of Christ.

    - **_Magnification_** – individuals would be led to come to appreciate value and adore the character of God through heart-felt genuine worship of Him in a local Church.
    - **_Ministry_** – individuals would be led to join a ministry where they can develop in bearing burdens and meeting needs according to the various relationships they will develop through the local Church.

    - **_Missions_** – individuals would be led into supporting the Church in sharing and defending the Christian faith.

V. **The Procedure for Checking Spiritual Development**
   A. Examine your thinking patterns (Romans 8:5-8, Romans 12:2).
   B. Examine the things that motivate you to live, to work, to serve, etc. (Matthew 6:21).
   C. Examine what you believe to be true about yourself (Proverbs 23:7a).
   D. Take notice of what you discuss consistently (Luke 6:45).
   E. Examine your behavior/attitudes (Galatians 5:19-22).
   F. Examine your lifestyle (2 Timothy 2:19, 2 Peter 1:1-10).
   G. Take notice of how you spend your time (Ephesians 5:8-17).
   H. Take notice of what you are producing in life (Luke 6:43-49, Galatians 6:7-10).
   I Examine the company you keep and their effect on you (1 Corinthians 15:33, Psalm 1:1-3).
   J. Take notice of what you are trying to accomplish or obtain (1 Timothy 6:6-12, Matthew 6:19-34).
   K. Take notice of how you relate to people (1 John 1:5-2:11).
   L Compare all these things to Christ only (Hebrews 12:1-3).

VI. The Pitfalls that Stifle Spiritual Development:
A. Consistently yielding to the tricks of Satan (1John 2:14-16).
B. Listening to worldly wisdom rather than to God's wisdom (James 3:13-18, Proverbs 8:1-36).
C. Holding grudges against others (1 John 2:9-11).
D. Wallowing in sin (1 John 2:1-6 Proverbs 28:13-14).
E. Not dealing with the issues of your heart (Jeremiah 17:9, Mark 7:14-23, Matthew 23:23-26).
F. Focusing on fleeting pleasures instead of pleasure evermore (Prov. 21:17, Ps 16:11).

VII. The Product of Spiritual Development
A. Consistently feeding on and developing in wisdom that comes from God (Hebrews 5:11-14, 1 Corinthians 2:1-3:2).
B. Evaluating things from a biblical perspective (1Corinthians 14:20).
C. Able to discern good and evil (Hebrews 5:11-14).
D. Pursuing the prize of becoming like Jesus Christ, anticipating the coming of Jesus Christ and the new heavenly body gained from Jesus Christ (Philippians 3:12-21).
E. Not caught up or manipulated by false doctrine (Ephesians 4: 13-14).
F. Love growing and increasing (Ephesians 4:11-16, 1Corinthians 13:4-8).
G. Walking consistently in love, joy, peace, patience, kindness, goodness, faithfulness, gentleness, and self control (Galatians 5:16-25).
H. Putting off a life of sin and putting on a life or right living through the power of God within (Ephesians 4:17-32, Romans 8:1-14).
I. Growing in moral excellence, knowledge, self-control, perseverance, godliness, brotherly kindness, and love (2 Peter 1:1-11, 1 John 2: 3-11).

VIII. The Plan for Spiritual Maturity
A. The Mission is to teach the fundamental doctrines of the Christian Faith
B. The Mission is to teach and train one how to walk in the fundamental disciplines of the Christian Faith
C. The Missions is to teach and train one how to walk in the fundamental duties of the Christian Faith
D. The Mission is to teach one how to live according to your demographic in the Christian Faith

Doctrines To know about	Disciplines How To:	Duties How To:	Demographics How To:
God Bible Christ Man Sin Salvation	Confess Sin Repent of Sin Study/Meditate on the Word of God	Bear Burdens Meet Needs Proclaim the Gospel	Function In Marriage As a Man As a Woman
Holy Spirit Church Last Things Angels Spiritual Leadership	Forgive Others Apply Truth Serve Others	Defend the Gospel Give Monetarily to support the Church	Function As a Senior Citizen As a Young Adult As a College Student
Spiritual Gifts Sanctification Old Testament New Testament Stewardship Judgment/ Rewards	Pray Worship Fast	Corporately Fellowship & Worship	Function As a Teenager As a Child

A Sample Discipleship Track for Spiritual Development and Maturity

Discovering the Fundamentals of Your Walk with God Track
- 100   Coming to Know and Walk With God by Nicolas Ellen
- 101   Dispenstationalism by Charles Ryie
- 102   Created for God's Glory by Jim Berg
- 103   Step by Step Through The Old Testament by Waylon Bailey & Tom Hudson

Developing in Your Walk With God Track
- 104   How People Change (Workbook) by Paul Tripp
- 105   Step By Step Through the New Testament by Thomas Lea & Tom Hudson
- 106   Changed Into His Image by Jim Berg
- 107   Basic Theology by Charles Ryie (The Doctrine of God, Christ, Holy Spirit, Bible)

Deepening your Walk with God Track
- 108   Pursuing Godliness through the Disciplines of the Christian Faith by Nicolas Ellen
- 109   Basic Theology by Charles Ryie (The Doctrine of Man, Sin, Salvation, Church)
- 110   Understanding and Developing a Christ Centered Life and Christ Centered Relationships by Nicolas Ellen
- 111   Grasping God's Word by J. Scott Duvall/J. Daniel Hays (How to study the Bible curriculum)

Discerning How to Live for God in this World Track
- 112   Understanding and Developing a Biblical View of Life by Nicolas Ellen
- 113   Decision Making in the Will of God by Gary Friesen
- 114   Basic Theology by Charles Ryie (The Doctrine of Angels, Demons, Last Things)
- 115   What a Way To Live by Tony Evans

Dealing with Your Relationship With Others Track
- 116   Relationships a Mess Worth Making by Paul Tripp
- 117   Helping People Change (Workbook) by Paul Tripp
- 118   Resolving Conflict God's Way by Jim Morris
- 119   Love the Answer by Rich Thomson

Denouncing the Works of the Flesh
- 120   With All Your Heart: Identifying and Dealing With Idolatrous Lust by Nicolas Ellen
- 121   Overcoming Sin and Temptation by John Owen, Kelly M. Kapic, Justin Taylor, John Piper
- 122   The Purifying Power of Living by Faith in Future Grace by John Piper
- 123   Essential Virtues: Marks of the Christ-Centered Life by Jim Berg

Disciplines of Ministry and Leadership Training
- 124   Elder Training Program
- 125   Pastoral Leadership Training Program
- 126   Deacon Training Program
- 127   Director of Ministry Training Program

128 Team Leader Training Program
129 Small Group Leader Training Program
130 Teacher Training Program
131 Biblical Counseling Training Program
132 Missions Training Program
133 Evangelism/Apologetics Training Program
134 Church Planting Training Program
135 Pre-Marital Discipleship Training Program
136 Apartment Ministry Training Program

Demographic Small Group Classes
Golden Age Class (Senior Citizens)
Men's Class
Women's Class
Marriage Class
Young Adult Class
College/Career Age Class
Youth Class
Middle School Class
Children's Class
Nursery Class

Section Ten

The Spiritual Warfare in the Sanctification Process

Key Point: The sanctification process will be challenged by your flesh, the world and Satan as he will seek to use his various schemes to short circuit you in the process. Biblical counseling helps individual to understand and work through these hindrances by helping them to learn and use God's tools to counteract the attacks. Biblical counseling must be a facilitator of helping people address these challenges or it will not be effective helping individuals accomplish the goal of transformation into the likeness of Christ.

I. The Danger of the Flesh

A. The flesh can be defined as the sin that indwells the human nature of man and propels man to practice evil in thoughts, desires, words, and actions (Romans 7:17, Galatians 5:19-21)

B. The flesh is dangerous because:
1. it wrestles and sets its desires against the Holy Spirit that dwells in us to lead us to contradict the will of God (Galatians 5:16-17).
2. there is no doing of good in the flesh (Romans 7:18)
3. it leads us to practice evil (Romans 7:19-21)
4. it leads us to be hostile towards God, to not subject ourselves towards God (Romans 8:7)
5. it puts us in a position where we cannot please God (Romans 8:7)
6. it leads one to death (Romans 8:6)
7. it wages war against our minds by appealing to us to fulfill the appetites of the mind in the wrong way (Romans 7:23).
8. it works through the physical body by appealing to us to fulfill natural bodily appetites in the wrong way (food, sex, sleep ect.) (Romans 7:23).
9. it leads us to be preoccupied with self, resulting in being devilish with others and distant from God (James 3:13-16)

C. God placed His Spirit within us to counteract our flesh. (Galatians 5:16-23; Romans 8:9-11).

D. God placed His Spirit within us to empower us to walk according to His will. (Romans 8:1-4).

II. The Deception of the World

A. The World – System can be described as the order of life based on satanic influence, human wisdom, and sensual desire; it contradicts God and His will (1 John 5:19, 1John 2:15-17).
B. The world is filled with things that appeal to our flesh. We must make decisions daily between God's will and the world's way. (1 John 2:15-17).
C. The world seeks to entice us to pursue the things in this life above the God of life resulting being friendly with world's system and acting as a enemy of God (James 4:1-10). We are enticed by things such as: money, material, movies, media, medications, achievements, affluence, approval, positions, power, pleasure, prominence
D. We are commanded and equipped to not love the world nor the things in the world (1John 2:15-17).

III. The Deceit of the Devil

A. The devil works through *False Religion* - organizations and churches that deny that salvation is through Jesus Christ (1Timothy 4:1; John 14:6; 1John 4:1-3).
B. The devil works through *Temptation* - enticing people away from God through the eyes, flesh, and mind (Genesis 3:1-24; James 1:12-15).
C. The devil works through *Accusations* - condemning people of sin to God (Revelations 12:10).
D. The devil works through *Fear* - trying to make people afraid to share, defend, and live the truth (1Peter 5:6-10; 1John 4:4; 2Timothy 1:6-10).

IV. The Devices of the Devil

A. Deception – leads people into error about God, life, self, relationships, government, and life issues through man-centered philosophies and logical sounding arguments based on the principles of this world's systems and the traditions of man promoted through demonic influence and doctrines of demons (2Corinthians 11:3, 14-15, 2Corinthians 4:4).
B. Division – seeks to separate people so that they will not work together in ways that promotes God's Kingdom; He draws people into selfish ambition , envy, and strife leading to disorder and every evil thing (James 3:13-16).
C. Doubt – seeks to get people to question the validity of God's Truth through various philosophies and logical sounding arguments promoted through demonic influence and doctrines of demons (Genesis 3:1-7).
D. Desires – appeals to our desires for food, comfort, sex, significance, satisfaction, security etc. to lead us into self-centeredness and disobedience to God in those areas; appeals to our corrupted nature to lead us to live for self, to live our own way resulting in being independent of God and His governing authorities; seeks to provide access to the things we treasure above God and His will so that we will sin to get them and sin when we don't get them (Matthew 4:1-11, James 1:13-17, Galatians 5:19-23).
E. Distraction – seeks to keep us preoccupied with matters that are not as important as single minded devotion to God; gets us focused on man's agenda instead of God's agenda (Mathew 16:21-23).

F. Discouragement – seeks to get Christians to lose hope in God and His will (1Peter 5:6-11).
G. Death – keeps people in slavery to him through the fear of death since he has power to murder (John 8:44, Hebrews 2:14-15).
H. Disbelief – seeks to lead people to ignore, deny, not believe, not trust, and resist the Truth about God, the Bible, themselves, the purpose of life, the reality of death and many other issues through various man-centered philosophies and logical sounding arguments promoted through demonic influence and doctrines or demons; this leads to sinful choices
I. and lifestyles that impact others in detrimental ways. (Genesis 3:1-11).
J. Dilution – seeks to lead us to blend in with the world's system by adopting their values, motives and trends to the point we have diluted our holiness with worldliness; this leads to lessening the power of our witness for Christ(James 4:4-7, 1John 2:15-17, 5:19).
K. Derailment – seeks to hinder our progress towards spiritual maturity and discipleship of others through various delays or disruptions in our lives (Romans 1:13, Revelation 2:10-11).

V. **The Defense of the Christian**
   A. There must be confession of self centeredness (Proverbs 28:13-14)
   B. Evil desires of the mind must be restrained and replaced with Godly desires for the mind. (Colossians 3:1-3)
   C. You must fulfill natural bodily appetites (i.e. food, sleep, and sex) in the right way and restrain from fulfilling these desire in the wrong way. (1 Corinthians 6:12-20, Proverbs 15:19)
   D. Learn to love others through serving instead of serving others to be loved. (Galatians 5:13)
   E. We must regulate what comes into our minds (Romans 12:2)
      1. Movies
      2. Media
      3. Music
      4. Mentalities
   F. We must repent of the sinful patterns we entertain in our minds (Ephesians 4:17-23)
      1. Antagonism
      2. Self Pity
      3. Worry
      4. Pride/Lust
   G. We must replace the sinful patterns with godly patterns to entertain in our minds (Philippians 4:8)
      1. True/Honorable thought patterns
      2. Right/Pure thought patterns
      3. Lovely/Good Repute thought patterns
      4. Excellent/Praiseworthy thought patterns
   H. We must resolve to present our bodies as a living sacrifice (Romans 12:2).
   I. We must resist the evil one by submitting to God (James 4:7).
   J. We must draw near to God expecting Him to draw near to us (James 4:8)

Take time this week and review what you need to put off and what you need to put on.

Sinful thoughts/desires I need to confess and repent of:	Godly thoughts/desires I need to replace them with:
Sinful words I need to confess and repent of:	Godly words I need to replace them with:
Sinful behavior and actions I need to confess and repent of:	Godly behavior and actions I need to replace them with:
Sinful relational patterns I need to confess and repent of:	Godly relational patterns I need to replace them with:
Areas I have neglected to serve God as He has designed me:	Areas I will serve God as He has designed me to serve:
Movies, Media, Music, Books, Relationships, Products, and Places that are leading me to partake in sin and ungodliness as I indulge them:	Movies, Media, Music, Books, Relationships, Products, and Places that I must replace them with in order to walk in holy and sacrificial lifestyle unto Jesus Christ:

Section Eleven

The Point of Choice

Key Point: At the end of the day man only has two choices; to be self-centered or God-centered. This drives every other issue in life man encounters. The more we choose to be self-centered the more we are held captive by our sin. The more we choose to be God-centered we are freed from sin but walk in slavery to God resulting in God's glory and our greatest good. The condition of our lives is determined by the choices we have made in life. Genuine biblical counseling helps individuals to understand this reality and to pursue choice of being God-centered.

I. **We choose to be God-Centered or Self-Centered**. (*Galatians 5:16-25*)
   (*See Illustration of Point I*)

   a. When we are God-centered we choose to live our lives for God resulting in doing things according to God's standards. (Psalm 119:105)

   b. When we are self-centered we choose to live our lives for ourselves resulting in doing things according to our own agenda. (2Timohty 3:1-4)

   c. When we choose to live for ourselves instead of living for God we will live in slavery to sin. (Proverbs 4:22).

   d. When we choose to live for God instead of living for ourselves we live in slavery to God (Romans 6:22).

Illustration of Point I.

God-Centered
Slave of God

Romans 6:22-But now having been freed from sin and enslaved to God, you derive your benefit, resulting in sanctification, and the outcome, eternal life.

Self-Centered
Slave of Sin

We have two choices in life. We either choose to be God-centered or self-centered. The more we choose to be self-centered the more we are held captive by our sin. The more we choose to be God-centered we are freed from sin but walk in slavery to God resulting in God's glory and our greatest good.

Proverbs 4:22 – His own iniquities will capture the wicked, and he will be he held with the cords of his sin.

Psalms 119:105 - Your word is a lamp to my feet and a light to my path.

2 Timothy 3:1-4-But realize this, that in the last days difficult times will come. For men will be lovers of self, lovers of money, boastful, arrogant, revilers, disobedient to parents, ungrateful, unholy, unloving, irreconcilable, malicious gossips, without self-control, brutal, haters of good, treacherous, reckless, conceited, lover of pleasure rather than lover of God.

Point of Choice

Graphics developed by Cathy Poulos from the presentation "Idols of the Heart," by Mark Dutton, NANC On-the-Road-Training, Track #1, Module #2, November 2003, Houston, TX.

The Point of Choice

II. **Our choices are driven by our thoughts.** *(Romans 8:5)*
(See illustration of Point II)

    a. When we are self-centered, our thoughts are dominated by lies and selfish ambition (James 3:13-16).

    b. As a result of those lies and selfish ambition, our thoughts tend to be driven and reduced to what we have been denied, what we believe we deserve, what we want, what we think we should have, or what we think we need. We become friendly with the world and unfriendly with God (James 4:1-10).

    c. When we are God-centered, our thoughts are dominated by truth and wisdom (James 3:17-18).

    d. As a result being dominated by truth and wisdom, our thoughts tend be driven by what God commands of us and how to live according to that; we focus on things such as what God promises to do for us and when to expect it. We tend to also focus on what God is doing for us and has done for us as well as what we can be doing for others and how to do it accordingly (James 3:17-18).

Illustration of Point II.

God-Centered   # Self-Centered

Inner Man ↔ Actions   Inner Man ↔ Actions

Point of Choice

Thinking

A mindset that God Wants Us to Develop

James 3:17-18 - The wisdom from above is first pure, then peaceable, gentle, reasonable, full of mercy and good fruits, unwavering, without hypocrisy. And the seed whose fruit is righteousness is sown in peace by those who make peace.

- ***A mind preoccupied with the truth of God's Word***

- ***A mind preoccupied with Godly wisdom***

A mindset that God Wants Us to *Avoid*

James 3:15-16 - But if you have bitter jealousy and selfish ambition in your heart, do not be arrogant and so lie against the truth. This wisdom is not from above, but earthly, natural and demonic.

- ***A mind preoccupied with lies***

- ***A mind preoccupied with selfish ambition***

Graphics developed by Cathy Poulos from the presentation "The Heart of Man as Presented in the Book of Psalms," by Mark Dutton, Co-Pastor of Faith Baptist Church, Lafayette, IN; NANC certified instructor.

The Point of Choice

III. **Our thoughts are motivated by the flesh (sin in our hearts) or by the Holy Spirit Romans 8:1-14** *(See illustration of Point III)*

    a. When our thoughts are motivated by the flesh (sin in our hearts), we are preoccupied with issues such as hedonism (preoccupation with whatever bring me pleasure apart from God), autonomy (independence from authority; not having to answer to any one), materialism (preoccupation with material things), and entitlement (believing I deserve whatever I want or pursue) dominate our thinking.

    b. This leads to further disobedience to God. We will see things such as anger, hatred, immorality, jealousy, abuse, cruelty, lying, selfish ambition, arrogance, rage, sarcasm or selfishness. This leads to a guilty conscience, a fear of God's judgment, and a desire to escape God's judgment resulting in trying to flee from the inevitable consequences of disobedience to God (2 Timothy 3:1-9, Proverbs 28:1).

    c. When our thoughts are motivated by the Holy Spirit we tend to be preoccupied with a desire to know Jesus Christ, to become like Jesus Christ, to be useful to Jesus Christ, the return of Jesus Christ, and the blessing in this life and the life to come from Jesus Christ our Lord.

    d. This leads to further obedience to God. We will see things such as humility, patience, peace, joy, self-sacrifice, kindness, goodness, mercy, love, faith, gentleness, self-control, and wisdom. This leads to a peaceful conscience, a confidence in the presence of God, and a desire to draw near to God resulting in drawing near to God (Galatians 5:22-25).

Illustration of Point III.

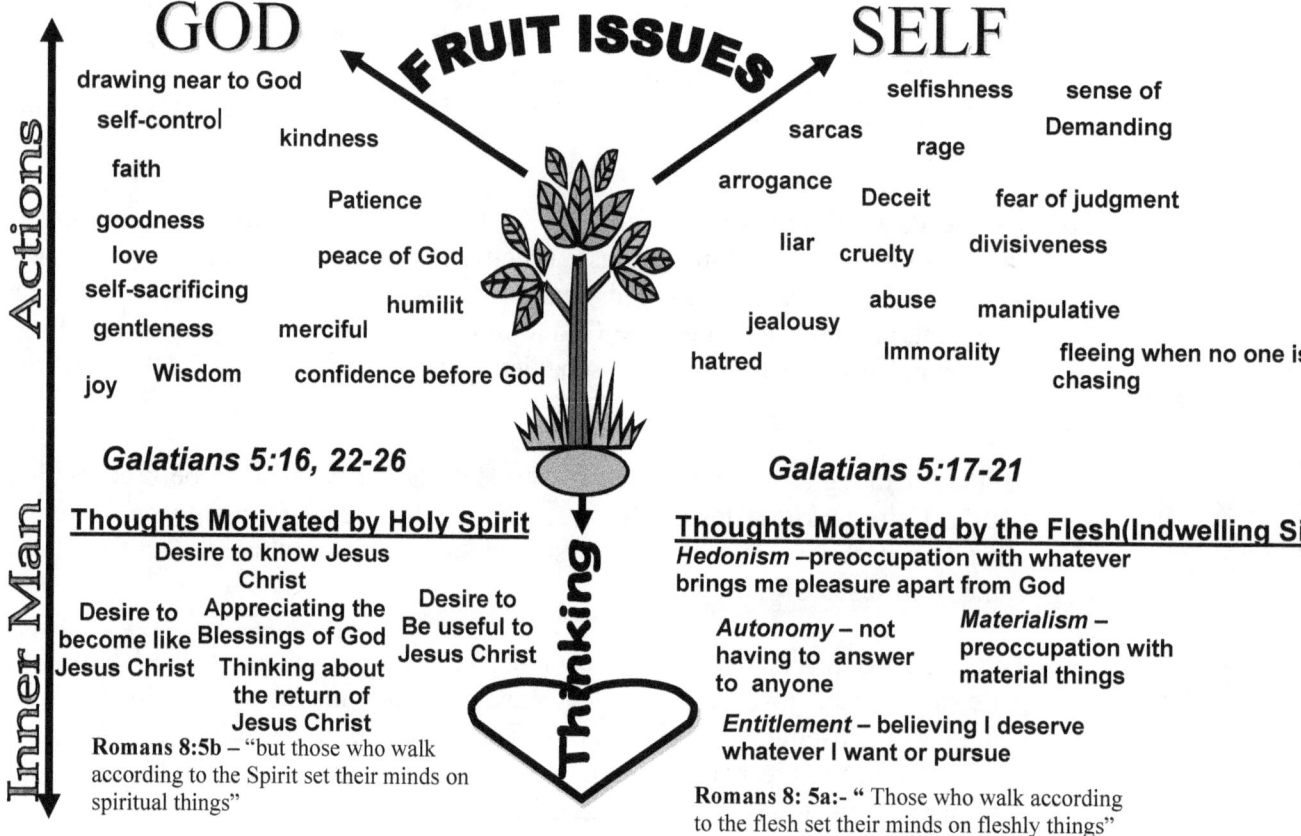

The Point of Choice

IV. **When our thoughts are driven by the flesh (sin in our hearts) we will begin to worship our desires, turning them into the lusts of our lives.** *(James 4:1-3)*
(See Illustration of Point IV and V)

    a. Our minds will be set on things below instead of things above leading us to make self interest a priority over God's will. We focus less and less on loving God and loving others; we focus more and more on using God and using others according to our self interest. (Philippians 3:17-19, James 3:13-4:3).

    b. Our desires will become preoccupations resulting in us looking for avenues to satisfy these desires we have started to worship. We look to any person, place, product, or perspective we believe will satisfy these desires we have started to worship above loving God and loving others (James 4:1-3).

    c. We will build our lives around these desires we have started to worship above loving God and loving others (Philippians 3:17-19).

    d. We will become servants of our flesh to satisfy these desires we have started to worship above loving God and loving others (Galatians 5:16-21).

Illustration of Point IV. & V.

To Be: Appreciated Great Loved Accepted Served In Charge Happy Approved Of: Understood Satisfied Significant Comfortable Safe Respected Held in High Regard Viewed as Competent

- To Have Influence
- To Never Hurt Again
- To Have Our Way
- To Have Control

Desires We Treasure and Worship above Loving God and Loving Others

Graphics by Audra Anderson

The Point of Choice

V. **As we make choices according to the desires we have begun to worship we will find ourselves on a path of difficulty and hard times** *(Proverbs 13:15) (See Illustration of Point IV and V).*

    a. We will become a slave to that which we pursue above loving God and loving others (2Peter 2:18-19).

    b. We will develop sinful habits that are hard to repent of and replace as a result pursing those desires we worship above loving God and loving others (Proverbs 5:21-22).

    c. We will reap negative consequences of our sinful habits in pursuit of those desires we worship above loving God and loving others (Galatians 6:7-8).

    d. We will have a negative effect on the lives of those around us as a result of pursuing those desires we worship above loving God and loving others (1Corinthians 5:1-6).

Illustration of Point IV. & V.

To Be: Appreciated Great Loved Accepted Served In Charge Happy Understood Satisfied Approved Of: Comfortable Safe Significant Respected Held in High Regard Viewed as Competent

Hearts: To Have Influence • To Never Hurt Again • To Have Our Way • To Have Control

Desires We Treasure and Worship above Loving God and Loving Others

Graphics by Audra Anderson

The Point of Choice

VI. **We must turn from a self-centered life to a God-Centered life through the Person, Power and Precepts of Jesus Christ.** *(Romans 13:8-14).*
(See Illustration of Point VI)

    a. We must identify the areas of our lives where we are dominated by lies, selfish ambition, hedonism, autonomy, materialism, entitlement, and lustful pursuits above loving God and loving others; We must identify where this is happening in our attitudes, intentions, desires words, actions, relationship patterns and service to God and confess and repent of these things accordingly (Proverbs 28:13-14).

    b. We must decide to make God a priority in all that we think, say and do (1Corinthians 10:31).

    c. The areas of lives where we are dominated by lies, selfish ambition, hedonism, autonomy, materialism, entitlement, and lustful pursuits, must be replaced with specific obedience to God accordingly in those areas (Ephesians 4:17-32, Colossians 3:1-25).

    d. In other words, we must guard our hearts from self-centeredness by walking in genuine love for God and love for others in our attitudes, intentions, desires, words, actions, relationship patterns, and service.

Illustration for Point VI.

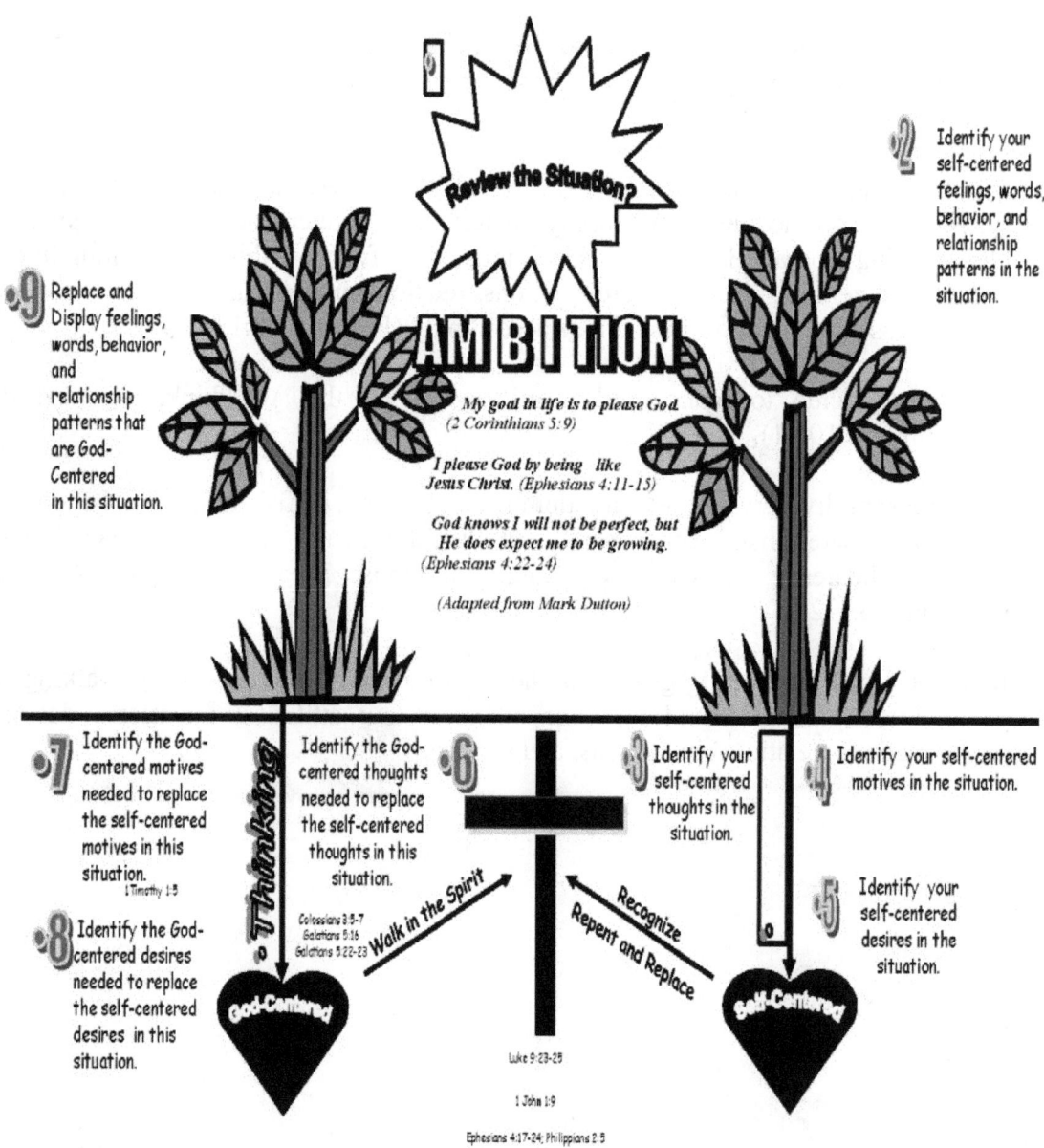

Adapted from curriculum presented in BC590s: Counseling Practicum, Dr. John Street professor, The Master's College, Santa Clarita, CA July 2004. Graphics by Cathy Poulos

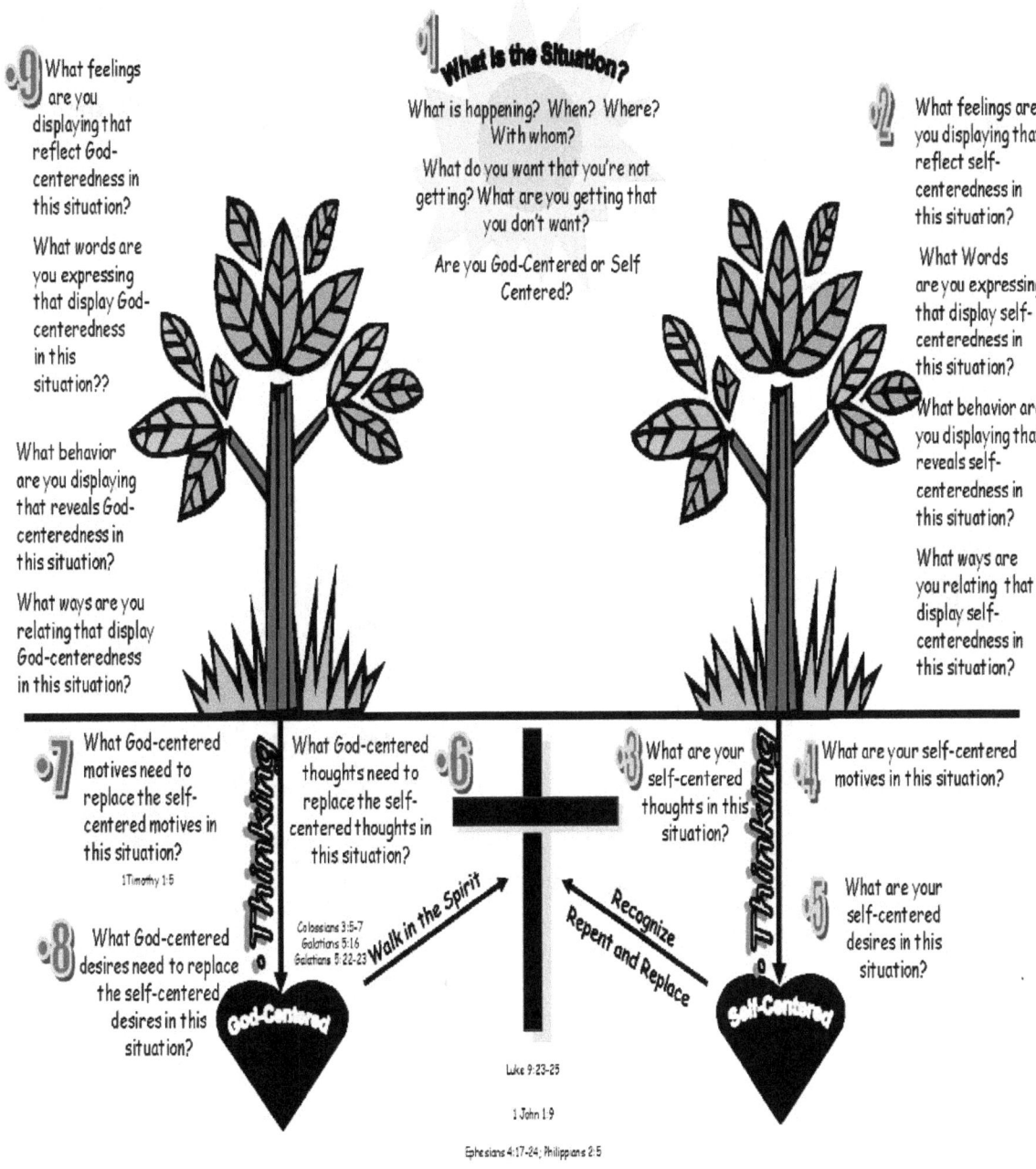

Graphics by Cathy Poulos

Illustration for point VI

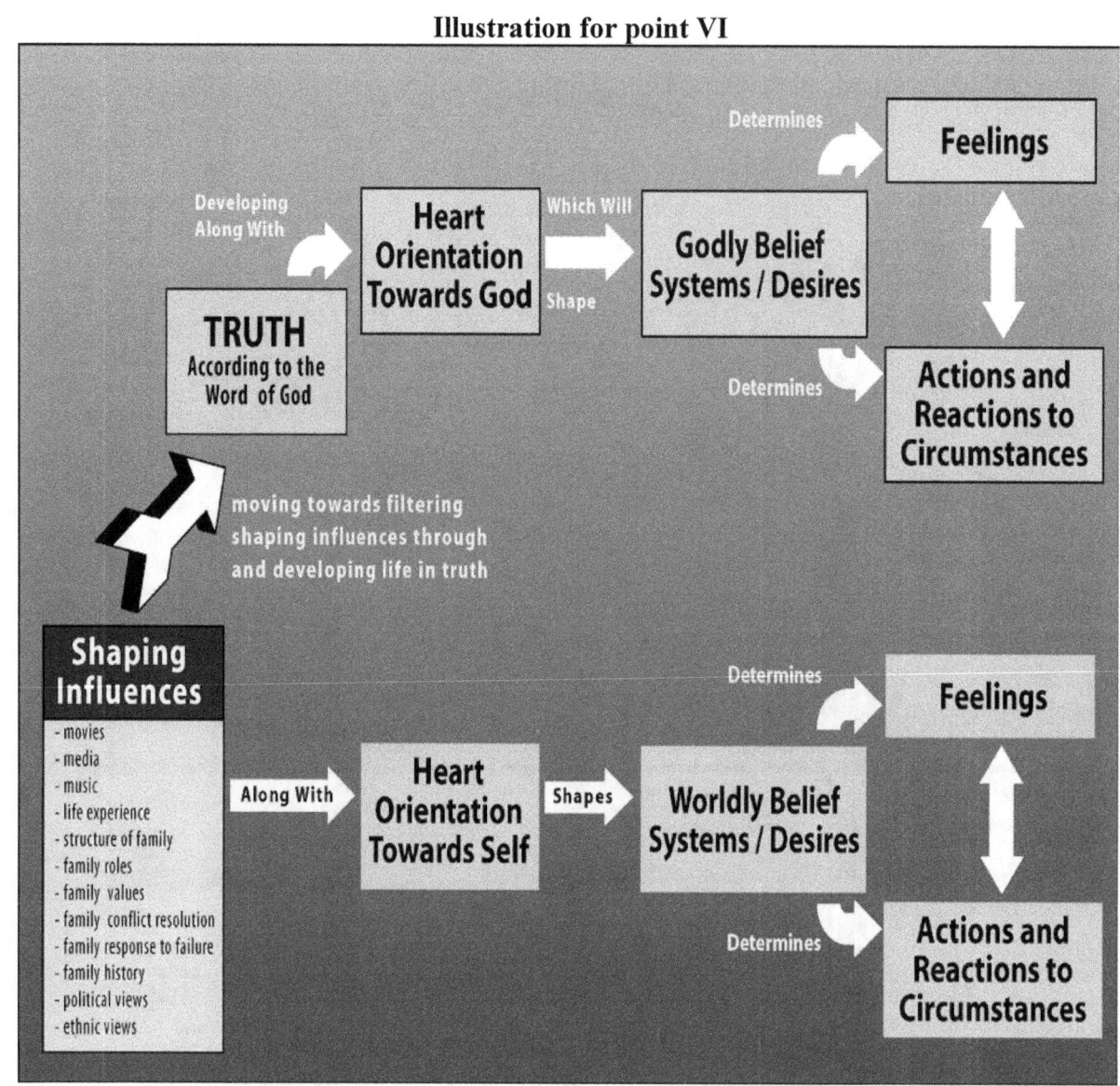

Graphics by Adrian Baxter

Two Choices Discussion Questions

1. When looking at the choices that you have made today, were you self-centered or God centered in your choices? Write down you findings.

   _____
   _____
   _____
   _____
   _____

2. Identify thought patterns you have which are rooted in lies and selfish ambition then identify thought patterns you have that are rooted in truth and godly wisdom. Explain how these thought patterns determined your choices above.

   _____
   _____
   _____
   _____

3. What desires have you allowed to become a form of worship resulting in further complications in your life?

   _____
   _____
   _____
   _____
   _____

4. What loving thoughts, motives, desires words, actions, relationship patterns and service do you need to walk in to replace the sin you are in?

   _____
   _____
   _____
   _____
   _____

The Purpose of Life
(2Corinthians 5:9,15)

Key Point: A Christ-Centered Life is a life that is devoted to knowing Jesus Christ intimately, becoming like Jesus Christ in character, conduct, and conversation, and being useful to Christ in all aspects of life. If we are going to understand and develop a Christ centered life we must understand ***The Purpose of Life.*** Genuine biblical counseling facilitates knowing the purpose of life and living according to that purpose.

I. The <u>Purpose</u> of Life (Why Do I exist):

   A. **To glorify God-to demonstrate** the greatness of His Character by functioning according to His design and will in all aspects of life.
   (Isaiah 43:7, Romans 11:36, Colossians 1:15-17, 1Corinthains 10:31, 2Corinthians 5:9,15, Matthew 5:14-16)

II. The <u>Objective</u> of Life (*What are the overarching goals I need to accomplish to fulfill my purpose?*):

   A. To know God intimately (*Relationship with God*) (John 17:3).
   B. To become like Jesus Christ to maturity in all aspects of life (*Sanctification in Jesus Christ*) (2Corinthians 3:18, Ephesians 4:11-16).
   C. To be useful to God (*Service for God*) (Ephesians 2:10, Romans 7:4, 1Peter 4:10-11).

III. The <u>Process</u> of Life (*What steps do I need to take to accomplish my goals to fulfill my purpose?*):

   A. Learn the Truth of God (2 Timothy 3:16, 2:15, Psalm 1:1-3, 119:104-105)
   B. Live the Truth of God you have learned (James 1:19-22, Psalm 119:101-102)
   C. Love others through the Truth of God you have learned and are living (John 13:34-35, 1Corinthians 13:4-8, Ephesians 4:16-17)

Section Twelve

A Biblical View and Response to Physical Illness and Christians on Psychotropic Drugs

Key Point: Illness is a by-product of the curse of sin from the fall of Adam and the result of sin in one's life, yet God can use it for His glory and our good. When you have an illness there is something wrong in the tissues of your body which can be proven by objective test. Mental illness is really not an illness but truly an issue of the immaterial heart that needs to be addressed through the Person of Jesus Christ, the Power of Jesus Christ and the principles of His Word. There may be physical issues that result from the spiritual problem that may require medication but the root issue cannot be cured through medication but only through submission to the Person and Power of Jesus Christ. Genuine biblical counseling operates by this premise. It does not promote medication where the Messiah is needed. Genuine biblical counseling discerns between pain that comes from the immaterial nature and pain that comes from the material nature.

I. The Biblical View of Physical Illness
   A. Illness exist because of the fall of Adam which resulted in the curse of sin on our lives leading to weak and frail bodies (Romans 5:12, 1Peter 1:24).
   B. Illness may occur due to unconfessed sin in ones' life (Psalm 32:1-4).
   C. Illness may occur because God is punishing an unbeliever (Exodus 15:26).
   D. Illness may occur because God is disciplining a believer (2Samuel 12:14-15).
   E. Illness may occur because God is seeking to bring about repentance (1Corinthtians 5:5).
   F. Illness may occur because God is using it to prevent a person from sinning (2Corinthains 12:7).
   G. Illness may occur as natural consequence of not taking care of one's body as designed (Proverbs 19:16).
   H. Illness may occur as a result of unbiblical thinking and actions (2Chronicles 26:19).
   I. Illness can be used by God to bring Glory to Himself (John 11:1-4).
   J. Illness can be used by God to expose the character of a person (Job 2:1-6).

II. Key Perspectives to consider for the person struggling with a Physical Illness
   A. There must be biblical understanding of physical illness (Romans 12:2).
   B. God has the physical illness under His sovereign control (Ecclesiastes 7:13-14).
   C. God will not allow physical illness to rise above what one can handle (1Corinthians 10:13).
   D. God will give what is needed so a person can function as God commanded in spite of the physical sickness (2Corinthains 9:8).

E. God wants a person to be victorious not a victim in their response to physical sickness (1Corinthains 15:57, Job 1:1-2:10).

III. An Approach to Help people with Physical Illness
    A. Help the counselee to see God's perspective on illness.
    B. Help the counselee to focus more on becoming like Christ as the primary goal and getting over the illness as the secondary goal.
    C. Teach the counselee how to use God's grace to function responsibly even when they feel horrible.
    D. Teach the counselee how to be thankful even when they feel terrible.
    E. Teach the counselee to focus on victory above relief.

The Distinction Between the Material and Immaterial Aspects of Man/Psychotropic Drugs (Insights from section adapted from <u>The Heart of Man and The Mental Disorders</u> by Rich Thomson)

Key Point: God's Word reveals that man's inner mental soundness is directly connected to those things for which he is responsible to God in his immaterial being, not with those things for which he is not responsible. (Human wisdom blames the brain for that which the Bible holds the heart responsible.)

IV. As created in the image of God, man, until death, is an inseparable unity of the material (body and brain) and the immaterial (heart- or soul and spirit).
    A. We have been designed with a mind which involves our thoughts, beliefs, understanding, memory, judgment, imaginations, discernment and conscience (See Proverbs 23:7, Romans 12:2-3, Romans 2:15-16, Mark 2:6, 2Corinthians 10:5).
    B. We have been designed with affections which involves our longings, desires, and feelings (See Psalm 20:4, Ecclesiastes 7:9, 11:9, Psalm 73:7, James 3:14, Hebrews 12:3, Joshua 14:8).
    C. We have been designed with a will which involves our ability to choose and determine action (See Deuteronomy 30:19, Joshua 24:15, Psalm 25:12, Ecclesiastes 2:4-8).
    D. Our mind, affections, and will, are the sum total of what we call the immaterial part of man (non-physical); The Bible generally uses the words soul, spirit, and heart when speaking of the immaterial aspect of man (See 1Corinthains 2:11, Roman 8:16, and Proverbs 4:23) (Sometimes the word soul is used to describe the whole person both material and immaterial (Acts 2:41)
    E. We have been designed with a physical body which is the home of the immaterial part of us (See 2Corinthains5:1-10, Philippians1:19-23, 1Corinthains9:27, and 1Corinthians 15:35-58).

F. The physical body and immaterial part of man are an inseparable union while man is alive on earth (See Genesis 2:7, 1Corinthians 15:35-38, Philippians 1:19-23).

G. We have been created as an eternal being that will live forever either in fellowship with God or in eternal damnation (See Luke 16:19-31, John 3:36, and Revelation 20:11-15).

H. We are accountable to God for our thoughts, words, and deeds (See 2Corinthians 5:10, Romans 14:10-12, and Ecclesiastes 12:13-14).

I. There is a distinction between the heart (soul and spirit) and the body; the heart (soul and spirit) is the real you and the body is the house in which the real you lives (See Genesis 1:26, 2 Corinthians 5:6-10, and Philippians 1:19-23).

V. Inside man's immaterial heart, is his individual personality which is not confined to his material body and brain. Our individual personality keeps on living even after we die (See Revelation 6:9-11, 1 Samuel 28:15-19, Luke 16:23-31; 9:28-31).

The Personality of Man

Read and analyze these Scriptures: Revelation 6:9-11, Luke 9:28-31, and make a list of things which are usually associated with man's brain but which in these instances are exhibited by people who are physically dead and have only their immaterial beings to account for them:

Characteristics normally tied to the brain of the living:
- A.
- B.
- C.
- D.
- E.
- F.
- G.
- H.
- I.
- J.
- K.
- L.
- M.
- N.
- O.

After doing the observation we find that many of those characteristics we assume are limited to the brain are not. Man's immaterial heart interfaces with his material brain while he functions on earth. After death many functions we associate with the brain continue in operation in man's immaterial being. The heart chooses and the brain is involved, but it is the heart that drives the choices not the brain. Man's immaterial heart is the control center of those things for which man is responsible to God. Inside man's immaterial heart is his individual personality which is not confined to his material body and brain. Our individual personality keeps on living even after we die.(Revelation 6:9-11, 1 Samuel 28:15-19, Luke 9:28-31)

V. Man's immaterial heart interfaces with his material brain in the area of thought. We need both the immaterial heart and material brain for the thought process to happen while we are living. Thought processes go on in the immaterial heart and the material brain while we are living. When we die thought processes continue in the immaterial heart.

    A. Daniel 2:28 (He was thinking thoughts in his material brain.)
    B. Daniel 2:30 (He was thinking thoughts in immaterial heart.)
    C. Song of Solomon 5:2 (Mind was awake while brain was unconscious.)

VII. Man's material body and brain may limit or expand his ability to think or experience things here on earth, but the body and brain do not determine those thoughts, words, or actions which man is responsible before God to choose in his immaterial heart. Some of us have great intellect, small intellect, and some are retarded but these issues do not effect the processes of the immaterial heart. Sin is not caused by the brain or brain chemicals but by the thought processes of the immaterial heart. Therefore, if there is an issue of sin in our lives we must blame the immaterial heart and not the material body and brain. Medicine may deal with the symptoms of the problem but not root issues (See Matthew 15:17-20, Mark 7:18-23, Proverbs 4:23, Philippians 4:8, Galatians 5:19-23, Proverbs 18:14, 1 Corinthians 10:13).

(Insights from this section adapted from <u>**The Heart of Man and The Mental Disorders**</u> by **Rich Thomson**)

VIII. Key Points to Consider about Christians on Psychotropic Drugs (psycho(mind) + tropic (affecting) = mind altering/affecting drugs)

A. Christians who are on psychotropic drugs may be focused more on feeling better through the medication than becoming better through the Biblical process of change.

B. Christians who use psychotropic drugs may not understand how to use the Bible to find God's solution to life's problem therefore they are left to secular understanding about their problems resulting in using psychotropic drugs as the solution.

C. Christians who use psychotropic drugs may be treated by professionals who deal only in psychotropic drugs to address the particular issues at hand.

D. Christians who use psychotropic drugs may believe that they cannot obey God when they feel bad; therefore they may believe that the only time they can be responsible is when they feel good by the use of medication.

E. Christians who use psychotropic drugs may have been told that there problems are based on physical conditions of the body that require medication.

F. Christians who use psychotropic drugs may not trust in the sufficiency of Scripture to handle their problems.

G. Christians who use psychotropic drugs may not understand or accept why and how God uses pain and trials to build character.

IX. Biblical Perspectives to consider about Christians and Psychotropic Drugs

A. The Bible is sufficient to provide everything we need for life and godliness which includes bad feelings that people try to address through psychotropic drugs instead of the Messiah and His Word (2Peter 1:1-11, 2Timothy 3:16-17).

B. God's goal for our lives is not that we live to feel better but that we live to become better through the Biblical process of Change (Ephesians 4:17-32, Colossians 3:1-17).

C. When there is no organic basis found for discomfort/ or pain you will find that unbiblical responses to life's situations are the core reasons for the discomfort/pain; therefore psychotropic drugs may deal with the pain of discomfort but it does not deal with the source of the discomfort (unbiblical responses) (Genesis 4:1-7, Romans 2:14-15).

D. Sin behavior and the bad feelings that follow do not come from organic problems of the body; sin behavior comes from the wickedness of the heart. The bad feelings that follow come from the conscience that stimulates the sense of guilt, apparently uncaused fear, and the desire to flee when no one is chasing. Therefore psychotropic drugs are not the cure the Messiah and His word are the cure (Matthew 15:11-20, Mark 7:20-23, 2Corinthians 5:11-17).

E. Psychotropic drugs will make you feel better but they will not help you to become better (Galatians 5:16-19-26, Genesis 4:1-7, Romans 7:4-8:15).

F. Medication is a great support but a terrible solution to non-organic problems (Proverbs 31:4-7).

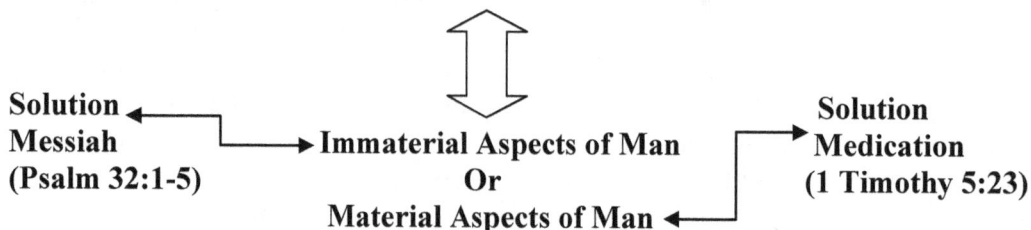

False Belief about medication and obedience

Pain < Obedience (Lesser the pain/ greater my obedience)

Pain > Obedience (Greater the pain /lesser my obedience)

Therefore, medication is necessary for me to obey God

False Conclusion: Medication brings relief of pain resulting in one feeling better and being able to obey as a result of feeling better from the medication.

Fallacy: One believes that the power to obey is caused by feeling better as the result of taking the medication.

Truth: The power to obey is determined by the Holy Spirit not feeling better as a result of taking medication. Pain or lack of pain does not determine the ability to obey. The ability to obey is determined by one's relationship and submission to God or lack thereof.
(Romans 8:1-15, Galatians 5:16-25)

X. An Approach to Help Christians on Psychotropic Drugs
A. Help the counselee identify the specific situations and problems that were happening to them, around them or through them that lead to the taking of psychotropic drugs.
B. Help the counselee identify the responses and reactions that took place from them in correlation to the specific situations and problems that lead to the taking of the psychotropic drugs.
C. Help the counselee to identify the negative feelings that arose and how they chose to handle those negative feelings in correlation to the specific situations and problems.
D. Help the counselee to identify their goal in the specific situations and problems (biblical or self-serving?)
E. Help the counselee identify their goal for taking the psychotropic drugs in the specific situations and problems.
F. Help the counselee to interpret life through Biblical categories in correlation to their specific situations and problems.
G. Help the counselee to apply Biblical principles to the specific situations and problems so that they will focus more on being like Christ instead feeling better in the crisis.

H. Help the counselee to focus on becoming a better person through application of biblical principles to the specific situations and problems instead feeling better in the specific situations and problems.
I. Coming off the medication is not the goal but helping the person to handle the specific situations and problem biblically is the goal.
J. As the counselee comes to see that they can handle the specific situations and problems through the power of God and the principles of His Word whether they feel bad or not they will begin to work on coming off the medication as a secondary goal as you have helped them to develop in the primary goal of the becoming like Christ and handling situations biblically as they walk for God and others.

(Information developed from the book ***The Christian Counselor's Medical Desk Reference*** by Robert D. Smith, MD.)

Section Thirteen

Why Do We Need Relationships?
(Ecclesiastes 4:9-12)

Key Point: Christ Centered Relationships are relationships that are primarily devoted to helping one another believe in Jesus Christ, become like Jesus Christ and belong to the community of Jesus Christ. If we are going to build Christ Centered Relationship we must ask and answer the question <u>***Why Do We Need Relationships?***</u> Genuine biblical counseling leads one into understanding the need for relationships and how to live in them in a Christ-centered way.

I. **God created people for Himself; He did not create people for our personal agendas (Romans 11:36)**

   A. God created people in His image (Genesis 1:26)
   B. God created people to demonstrate the greatness of His Character (Isaiah 43:7)
   C. God created people to know Him, to worship Him and to be useful to Him in the process of building a God-Honoring community and to be ambassadors for this God- Honoring Community (Jer 9:23-24, Deu 6: 13-15, 2Tim 2:20-21, Ephesians 4:1-17, 2Corinthains 5:15-21)

II. **We should not use each other as avenues to satisfy our personal agendas (Philippians 2:3-4)**

   A. We should not use people as avenues to make us happy (Jeremiah 17:5-6)
   B. We should not use people as avenues to make us secure (Jeremiah 17:5-6)
   C. We should not use people as avenues to make us feel good about ourselves (Proverbs 29:25)

III. **Our goal is to love others as we enjoy them instead of enjoying them as we consider if we will love them** (*people are to be loved not used*) **(Matthew 22: 34-40)**

   A. We should seek to build up others for Jesus Christ instead of using them to satisfy our personal preferences (Romans 15:2-3)
   B. We should seek to serve others for Christ instead seeking them to serve us for ourselves (Romans 12:9-13)
   C. We should not be looking for love but looking to love (Romans 13: 8-14)

IV. **There are Six key hindrances to loving others as we enjoy them: (Insights Adapted from Relationships by Tim Lane and Paul Tripp)**

   A. Self centeredness – living as if the world to revolves around you/ Self Rule – living by your own authority instead under the authority of God
   B. Self Taught- living by your own source of wisdom and truth/ Self Righteousness – living by your standard of what is right
   C. Self Sufficiency – living as if you are able to support yourself and sustain yourself apart from God/ Self Satisfaction – seeking to find satisfaction for self in people or in things apart from God and His will

V. **We need relationships to help us be more productive in life to God's Glory (v9)**

   A. We need each other so that we may help each other function in spiritual maturity in all aspects of life (Ephesians 4:11-16)
   B. We need each other so that we may strengthen areas of weakness in each other's lives (Romans 15:1-10)
   C. We need each other so that we may sharpen each other's perspectives of life to grow in righteousness (Proverbs 27:17)

VI. **We need relationships to help lift us up when we fall (v10)**
   A. We need each other to help recover from the consequences of poor decisions (Galatians 6:2)
   B. We need each other to help confess and repent of sin (Galatians 6:1-2)
   C. We need each other to help replace our sin with right living (Galatians 6:1-2)

VII. **We need relationships to comfort us in times of afflictions (v11)**
   A. We need encouragement from one another in hard times (Romans 12:15)
   B. We need tangible support from one another in hard times (Proverbs 17:17)
   C. We need wise counsel from one another in hard times (Proverbs 20:5)

VIII. **We need relationships to help us resist the temptations we will face in life (v12)**
   A. We need to help one another stay away from people who lead us into sin (Jude 1-25
   B. We need to help one another stay away from places that lead us into sin (Hebrews 3:12-13)
   C. We need to help one another stay away from products that lead us into sin (Hebrews 3:12-13)

IX. **In order to apply this insight there are 11 Key things we need to focus on:**
   (Insights adopted from the book <u>Relationships</u> by Tim Lane and Paul Tripp)

   A. I must have a sober assessment of myself, seeing myself as Child of God being transformed into the image of Christ
   B. I must embrace and worship the Creator above the Creation finding my satisfaction in Him
   C. I must see others as either saved or unsaved and in need of the grace and mercy of God
   D. I must embrace the fact that who I am is based on who God has called me to be
   E. I must embrace the fact that the creation was not designed to define who I am
   F. I must value Christ above what I want from others and what I want to see in others
   G. I must stop trying to recreate others into my image and for my personal preferences
   H. I must look at others and see the image of God
   I. I must look at others and see the plan of God and not a view man as a hindrance or help to my agenda
   J. I must not seek to motivate others to please me
   K. I must seek to motivate others to please God
   L. (Concept Adapted from Steve Viars Sermon Called "Why Do We Need People" 10/03 NANC Conference)

The Four Kinds of Human Relationships
(Proverbs 27:5-6)

A. Sometimes our relationships can be **open and unloving**. (v5)
   1. Rebuking others without respect.
   2. Exposing sin with rudeness.
   3. Exposing character flaws with harshness.
   4. Speaking truth with no love.

B. Sometimes our relationships can be **closed and loving**. (v5)
   1. Appreciative but not expressing it.
   2. Concerned but not showing it.
   3. Having praise in heart but not expressing it.
   4. Desiring the highest good of others but not expressing it.

C. Sometimes our relationships can be **open and loving**. (v6)
   1. Rebuking in love
   2. Spending quality time.
   3. Speaking the truth in love/giving encouragement.
   4. Meeting needs and bearing burdens.

D. Sometimes our relationships can be **closed and unloving**. (v6)
   1. Talking behind someone's back instead of to them
   2. Insincere favors or gifts.
   3. Flattery

       4. Uncooperative

Conclusion: An open loving relationship can be expressed to others in many ways at the right time, in the right way and in the right circumstance (Proverbs 25:11, Colossians 3:12-13).

  E. All open and loving relationships should begin with sincere ***confession*** of sin when you have sinned against others (Luke 17:3-4).
    1. Acknowledging the specific sin in words you have committed against them and seek forgiveness.
    2. Acknowledging the specific sin in actions you have committed against them and seek forgiveness.
    3. As much as it depends on you seek to be at peace with the individual.
    4. If it is not clear sin, there is no need to acknowledge as sin because clear sin not denying personal preferences is be acknowledged; If you did not keep your word in doing something then the clear sin is not keeping your word.

  F. All open and loving relationships should then proceed to ***turning away*** from those specific words and actions confessed (Proverbs 28:13).
    1. There should be a turning away from the specific sinful words.
    2. There should be a turning away from the specific sinful actions.
    3. This should be done with the intent to glorify God.
    4. This should be done considering the damage the sin caused the relationship.

  G. All open and loving relationships should then proceed to speaking loving ***words*** (Ephesians 4:29).
    1. Focus on speaking words of praise to others with sincerity.
    2. Focus on speaking words of encouragement with sincerity.
    3. Focus on speaking words of appreciation with sincerity.
    4. Focus on speaking words of rebuke with sincerity.

  H. All open and loving relationships should then proceed to walking in loving ***actions*** (Romans 13:8-14).
    1. Focus on comforting others with sincerity.
    2. Focus on bearing others burdens with sincerity.
    3. Focus on appropriate touch of others with sincerity (kiss, hug, etc.).
    4. Focus on supporting others accordingly.

  I. All open and loving relationships should follow the Biblical Mandate according to the relationship (1Cor13:4-7).
    1. Husband/Wife (Eph. 5:18-33, Col. 3:18-19, I Peter 3:1-12)
    2. Children (Eph. 6:1-2, Col. 3:20)
    3. Parent (Eph. 6:4, Col. 3:21, Deut. 6:6-9, Prov. 22:6)
    4. Friends (Prov. 27:5-6, Prov. 17:17, Prov. 27:9, Prov. 18:24)
    5. Others (I Peter 3:8-12, Rom. 12:9-21, Gal. 6:1-10)
    6. Leaders (I Tim. 4:16, Heb. 13:7, 17; I Peter 5:5, I Tim. 5:17-22, Luke 6:40)

7. Employer/Employee (Eph. 6:5-9, I Peter 2:18-29)
8. Government (Rom.13:1-2, I Peter 2:13-17)
9. Enemies (Luke 6:27-36)

J. As Ambassadors for Jesus Christ, Christians are to build open and loving relationships with unbelievers to present the message of reconciliation (2Corinthians 5:20-21).
   1. As ambassadors, Christians seek to persuade unbelievers to accept the reality of the judgment of Christ to come on sin.
   2. As ambassadors, Christians seek to explain to unbelievers the reality that all have sinned and need to be saved from the coming judgment of Christ to come on them as a result of their sin.
   3. As ambassadors, Christians seek to persuade unbelievers to repent of sin and be reconciled to God through faith in the person and work of Jesus Christ resulting in being saved from the penalty, power and soon presence of sin unto a genuine relationship with God where they are made righteous as result Christ taking their penalty and punishment for sin; leading to knowing Jesus Christ, becoming like Jesus Christ, and being useful to Jesus Christ.
   4. Ambassadors are motivated by God's love which leads them to understand that their life is to be lived for Christ since He died for them; This leads them to see people according to their condition before God(saved or not saved) This leads them to see people as new creatures in Christ or in need of reconciliation in Christ.

K. As Builders for Jesus Christ, Christians are to build open and loving relationship with other believers to help believers develop in maturity in Christ (Ephesians 4:11-16).
   1. Saints are to work on building each other up to the unity of the faith- helping all saints to reach oneness in our faith in Jesus Christ; helping all saints reach the same level of trust in Jesus Christ.
   2. Saints are to work on building each other up in unity in the knowledge of the Son of God- helping all saints reach the same level of full, correct, and precise knowledge of Christ in all aspects resulting in waling in maturity in all aspects of life as Christ would.
   3. Saints are to keep other saints from being led astray and unstable in their lives as a result of listening to every wind of doctrine-different teachings of religious quacks and philosophers.
   4. Saints are to keep other saints from being led astray and unstable in their lives as a result of the trickery of men -con artist of the faith; men who play on your neediness or greediness.

1 CORINTHIANS 13:4-8

The Various Roles I have in Life	Loving Thoughts I should have towards others in this role	Loving Words I should have towards others in this role	Loving Service I should do towards others in this role	Any other things I can think of
Father / Husband				
Wife				
Child				
Brother				
Sister				
Aunt				
Niece				
Nephew				

THE VARIOUS ROLES I HAVE IN LIFE	LOVING THOUGHTS I SHOULD HAVE TOWARDS OTHERS IN THIS ROLE	LOVING WORDS I SHOULD HAVE TOWARDS OTHERS IN THIS ROLE	LOVING SERVICE I SHOULD DO TOWARDS OTHERS IN THIS ROLE	ANY OTHER THINGS I CAN THINK OF
Grandfather				
Grandmother				
Cousin				
Mother-in-law				
Father-in-law				
Son-in-law				
Daughter-in-law				
Friend				

The Various Roles I Have in Life	Loving Thoughts I should have towards others in this role	Loving Words I should have towards others in this role	Loving Service I should do towards others in this role	Any other things I can think of
Co-worker				
Employer				
Employee				
Enemy				
Neighbor				
Authority figure				
Subordinate				

Section Fourteen
Understanding the Church

Key Point: God has made His church the pillar of truth. When we look at the Church we should see the character of God in the Church. If a person does not understand God's purpose for the Church, he may misunderstand his role in the Church. Therefore, we must learn these things that we may honor God in our church. Counseling that is God-honoring functions as an instrument of the church. The role of counseling is directly related to the work of the church just as the work of the church is directly related to the work God. No counseling ministry of church can fulfill the mission of the church if it is does understand and practice evangelism when necessary. Moreover, the counseling ministry of the church cannot fulfill the mission of the church if it does not understand and practice the work of discipleship accordingly. As the church is doing evangelism and discipleship, we should see her counseling ministry functioning in evangelism and discipleship as well. The counseling ministry should not be a ministry of recovery. Rather, the counseling ministry should be a ministry of repentance and transformation.

I. What is the Church?

A. **Universal** – the sum total of all who have accepted Jesus Christ as Lord and Savior which is also called the Body of Christ; Men and women who are called out of the world and united with God (1Corinthians 1:1-2, 1Corinthians 12:27, 1Peter 2:9).

B. **Local** – A group of believers who are connected together geographically in an area of town so that they may do God's will (1Timothy 3:14-16).

II. What is the function of the Church?

   A. To worship God in spirit and in truth (John 4:23-24, Philippians 3:1-3).
   B. To instruct believers in the Scripture so they function as God intended (Ephesians 4:11-17, Matthew 28:18-20).
   C. To fellowship with one another (Acts 2:42-43, Hebrews 10:23-25)
   D. To evangelize those who need to be saved (2Corinthians 5:20, Matthew 28:18-20).
   E. To bear one another's burdens (Galatians 6:2).
   F. To meet one another's needs (1John 3: 17-18, James 2:14-17).

III. What Should the Church Display?

A. The Church should display unity (1Corinthians 1:9-10, Philippians 1:27-2:11).
B. The Church should display love (1Corinthians 13:1-7, John 13:33-34).
C. The Church should display holiness (1Peter 1:14-16).
D. The Church should display truth (1Timothy 3:14-16).

IV. Who is responsible for taking care of the local Church?

A. *Pastors/Teachers* - given the responsibility for shepherding the Body of Christ. They are responsible for:
   1. Teaching the body biblical truth.
   2. Leading the Church in a direction that fulfills the Kingdom agenda.
   3. Watching over (shepherding) those in the local Church.
   4. Maintaining order, unity and holiness within the body.
   5. Overseeing all aspects of the Church.
   6. Scripture references: Ephesians 4:11-17, Acts 20:28, Hebrews 13:17, Romans 16:17-20, 1Corinthians 5:1-13, Matthew 18:15-20, 1Timothy 3:1-7).

B. *Elders*- given the responsibility for shepherding the Body of Christ. They are responsible for:
   1. Teaching the body biblical truth.
   2. Leading the Church in a direction that fulfills the Kingdom agenda.
   3. Watching over (shepherding) those in the local Church.
   4. Maintaining order, unity and holiness within the body.
   5. Overseeing all aspects of the Church.
   6. Scripture References: Ephesians 4:11-17, Acts 20:28, Hebrews 13:17, Romans 16:17-20, 1Peter 5:1-4, Titus 1:5-9).

C. *Deacons* – given the responsibilities of helping the Pastor and Elders through addressing the practical or tangible needs of the body of Christ within the local Church (Acts 6:1-7, 1Timothy 3:8-13).

V. What are some of the systems by which the local Church functions?

A. *Episcopal System* – A bishop is given authority over a group of Churches. He governs them accordingly. This system is generally found in Methodist, Episcopal, Roman Catholic, and Lutheran denominations.

B. *Presbyterian System* – Elders in plurality govern the church and are responsible for all aspects of the church. This system is generally found in Presbyterian Churches, Bible Churches and other non-denominational churches.

C. *Congregational System* – the congregation has authority and makes the decisions accordingly through voting. They designate and assign the Pastors and all other leaders accordingly by voting. This system is generally found in Evangelical Free, Baptist, and Lutheran denominations.

D. **Note:** We may see aspects of all styles in any given Church or groupings of Churches.

VI. What is my role as a member of the local Church?

A. You are to bear burdens of others (Galatians 6:2).
B. You are to meet the needs of others (1John 3:17-18).
C. You are to use your spiritual gifts accordingly (1Peter 4:10-11, Romans 12:3-8).
D. You are to maintain unity within the church (Ephesians 4:1-3).
E. You are to love others accordingly (1Timothy 1:5, Romans 12:8-21).
F. You are to be a disciple and to make disciples of Christ (Matthew 28:18-20, Luke 9:23-
G. 26).
H. You are to give monetarily to support the work of the Church (2Corinthians 9:6-15).
I. You are to conduct yourself in a manner that is holy and honorable (1Peter 1:13-16,
J. Romans 12:17).

VII. What are the signs that a local Church is functioning properly?

A. There will be many spiritually mature people (Ephesians 4:11-17).
B. There will be an atmosphere of love (John 13:33-34).
C. There will be needs met and burdens bared on a consistent basis (Acts 4:32-33).
D. There will be a consistent number of people becoming disciples of Christ(Acts 2:42-47)
E. There will be an atmosphere of true worship, prayer and holiness (John 4:23-24, 1Timothy 2:1-8).

VIII. What is the big picture?

A. God is *saving souls* from hell and *maturing saints* into the image of Christ (Ephesians 2:1-10, 2 Corinthians 3:17-18).
B. God is using *the Church through evangelism and discipleship* to save souls from hell and mature saints into the image of Christ (Matthew 28:18-20, 2Corinthians 5:15-20, Ephesians 4:11-17).
C. God is using *individuals within the church through their spiritual gifts* which results in burdens being beared, needs being met, and truth being proclaimed. This results in evangelism and discipleship taking place, which results in souls being saved from hell and saints being matured into the image of Christ (Romans 12:3-8, 1 Peter 4:10-11, Ephesians 4:15-16).
D. Therefore as members of the Church we are to be *anticipating the return of Christ* through living righteously in Christ and purifying ourselves from sin in thoughts, words, and actions (1John 3:1-3, Philippians 3:1-21).

The Essential Point of The Church

Through work of evangelism and discipleship, to lead individuals into salvation, sanctification, and service resulting in a community that _believes_ in Jesus Christ that _belongs_ to the community of Jesus Christ that _becomes_ like Jesus Christ.

Step 1 — Salvation

Through a literal crucifxtion on on the Cross, death, burial and resurection from the dead as result of that literial cricifixtion, Jesus Christ paid the penalty of the sin debt that all mankind owes to God. You will be saved from the penalty of sin the power of sin and one day the presence of sin and saved unto a genuine relationship with God if you repent of sin and put a genuine trust/belief in Jesus Christ as Savior from the penalty of your sin and Lord of your life

Step 2 — Sanctification

As result of one's salvation, one should seek to turn from Self reliance, Sin and God replacements to develop in Chrislike Character, Conduct, and Conversation through genunine fellowship and obedience to Jesus Christ as He uses His, power, people and circumstances to tranform you unto His Image

Step 3 — Service

There must be a commitment to serve as an Ambassodor to Unbelievers (Evangelsim) and to serve as a Builder to Believers (Discipleship) using your Spiritual gifts to bear burdens, meet needs and proclam the truth which will resulit in learning to love people, to know what their issues are, to speak the truth in love as it relates to those issues and to lead them to do some thing about those issues as it relates to either salvation or sanctification

Summation

Through your Salvation, Sanctifiction, and Service, God will use you to bring People:
- To Believe in Jesus Christ
- To Belong to the Community of Jesus Christ (The Body of Believers)
- To Become like Jesus Christ through His Community (The Body of Believers)

The Essential Practice of The Church

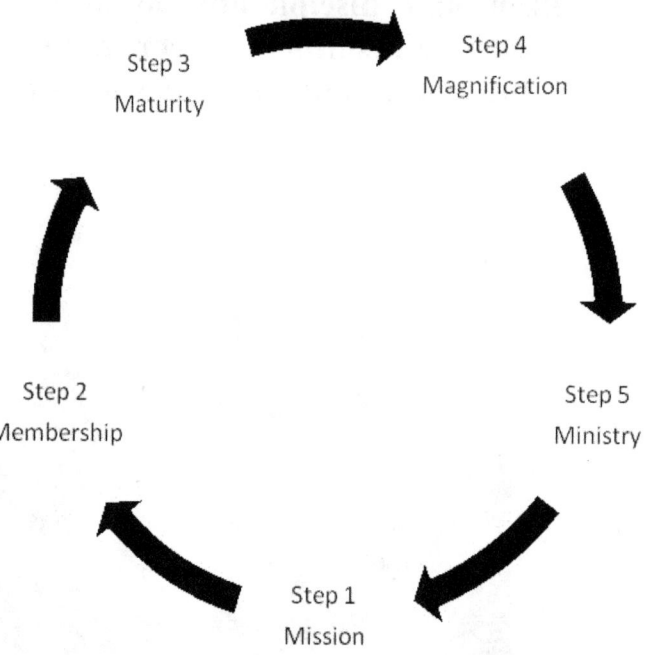

Step 1 Mission – going out into the community, city, state, country, and world to make Disciples of Jesus Christ

Step 2 Membership – building genuine relationships with one another within the local body and bringing those people we have lead to become disciples through our evangelism into genuine relationship with us and others within the local body of Christ; holding one another accountable to live accordingly in Jesus Christ

Step 3 Maturity – teaching the members within the local assembly who God is, what He requires, who we are in Christ, how to function according to our new position, power, purity, purpose, and passion in Jesus Christ; how to put off a life of sin and put on life of righteousness according to our faith in Jesus Christ; helping members develop in the application of these things; teaching members the doctrines, disciplines, duties, and demographics of the Christian faith and helping them develop in application of these things accordingly

Step 4 Magnification – teaching members how to embrace and to genuinely worship God according to who He is in character and what He has done; helping them grow in true worship

Step 5 Ministry - helping members to discover their spiritual gifts, leading them to use their spiritual gifts to bear burdens and meet needs of one another within the local assembly; helping members to become builders of the body of Christ and ambassadors to the world for Christ

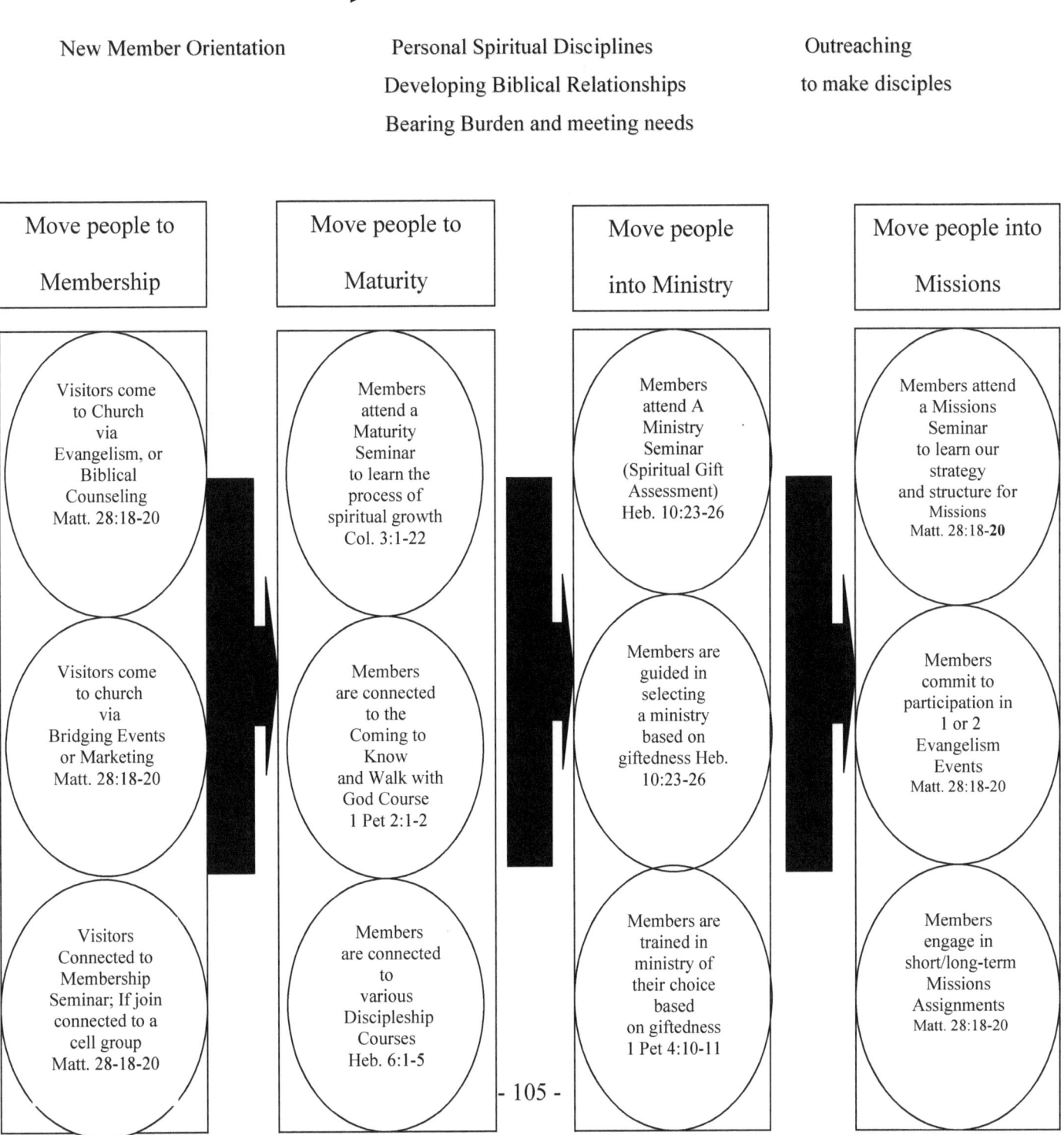

The Essential Precepts of The Church

Doctrines To know about	Disciplines How To:	Duties How To:	Demographics How To:
God Bible Christ Man Sin Salvation	Confess Sin Repent of Sin Study/Meditate on the Word of God	Bear Burdens Meet Needs Proclaim the Gospel	Function In Marriage As a Man As a Woman
Holy Spirit Church Last Things Angels Spiritual Leadership	Forgive Others Apply Truth Serve Others	Defend the Gospel Give Monetarily to support the Church	Function As a Senior Citizen As a Young Adult As a College Student
Spiritual Gifts Sanctification Old Testament New Testament Stewardship Judgment/ Rewards	Pray Worship	Corporately Fellowship & Worship	Function As a Teenager As a Child

BIBLIOGRAPHY

Books

Adams, Jay. *A Theology of Christian Counseling*. Grand Rapids: Zondervan, 1979.

Adams, Jay. *Winning the War Within.* Woodruff, SC: TimelessTexts,1989.

Augustus Hopkins Strong. *Systematic Theology: A Compendium and Commonplace-Book Designed for the Use of Theological Students.* Rochester, NY: Press of E. R. Andrews, 1886.

Berg, Jim. *Taking Time to Quiet A Noisy Soul.* Greenville, SC: BJU Press, 2005.

Bridges, Jerry. *Trusting God: Even When Life Hurts*. Colorado Springs: NaviPress, 1988.

Colsen, Charles. *How Now Shall We Live?.* Carol Stream Il: Tyndale Publishers, 1999.

Easton, M.G. *Easton's Bible Dictionary* (Logos Research System; reprint). Oak Harbour, WA: Public Domain, 1996.

Edwards, Dwight. *Experiencing Christ Within.* Colorado Springs: WaterBrook Press, 2002.

Ferguson, Sinclair. *The Christian Life: A Doctrinal Introduction.* London: Hodder and Stoughton, 1981.

Fitzpatrick, Elyse. *Idols of the Heart*. Phillipsburg: P & R Publishing Company, 2001.

Grudem, Wayne. Systematic Theology. Leicester: Inter-Varsity Press, 1994.

Hodge, A.A. Providence, in *Outlines of Theology.* Carlisle, PA: The Banner of Truth Trust, 1983.

Hodge, Charles. *Commentary on 1 & 2 Corinthians*. Edinburgh: Banner of Truth Trust, 1974.

Ingram, Chip *The Invisible War.* Grand Rapids, Michigan: Baker Books, 2006.

J. B. Lightfoot, J.B. *The Epistles of St. Paul III: The First Roman Captivity, Saint Paul's Epistle to the Philippians.* London: Macmillan, 1896.

MacArthur, John. *The MacArthur Study Bible*. Nashville: Word Publishing, 1997.

Noebel, David. *Thinking like a Christian (Teaching Textbook).* Nashville: Broadman–Holman Publishers, 2002.

Piper, John. *God's Passion for His Glory*. Wheaton, Il: Crossway Books, 1998.

Powlison, David. *Seeing With New Eyes*. Philipsburg, NJ: P&R Publishing, 2003.

Ryrie, Charles C. *Basic Theology*. Wheaton: Victor Books, 1995.

Sire, James. *The Universe Next Door 4th Edition.* Downers Grove, Il: InterVarsity Press USA, 2004.

Smith, Robert. *Medical Desk Reference*. Stanley, NC: Timeless Texts, 2000.

Thomson, Rich. *The Heart of Man and The Mental Disorders.* Alief, Tx: Biblical Counseling Ministries, 2004.

Tozer, A.W. *The Knowledge of the Holy*. New York: Harper Collins, 1961.

Tripp, Paul. *Relationships: A Mess Worth Making.* Greensboro, NC: New Growth Press, 2006.

Walvoord, John. *The Holy Spirit*. Grand Rapids: Zondervan, 1965.

Walvoord, John F. *Jesus Christ Our Lord*. Chicago: Moody Press, 1969.

Wiersbe, Warren. *Bible Exposition Commentary*. Victor, 1989.

Wuest, Kenneth S. *Wuest's Word Studies from the Greek New Testament : For the English Reader*. Grand Rapids: Eerdmans, 1997.

Notes

Dutton, Mark. *Idols of The Heart and The Heart of Man as Presented in the Book of Psalms Notes.* NANC Training, 2003.

Patten, Randy. *What Makes Biblical Counseling Unique Notes.* NANC Training, 2009.

Shockley, Paul. *"Know the Truth (Lecture 3)"*. Notes from Biblical World view Course at the College of Biblical Studies Houston, Texas

Street, John. *BC 590 Counseling Practicum Notes .* Masters College Santa Clarita, Ca. 2004.

Viars, Steve. *Why Do We Need People? Sermon*. NANC Conference, 2003.

Websites

"What is Sanctification?" [on-line]; accessed 5 November 2009; available from http://gotquestions.org/sanctification.html; Internet.

www.ingramcontent.com/pod-product-compliance
Lightning Source LLC
Chambersburg PA
CBHW081257170426
43198CB00017B/2825